MW01258814

THE AGE OF CHIVALRY

PART 3

Other volumes of The Age of Chivalry

Part 1 – The 8th to the 15th century

Helmets and mail

Tournaments and heraldic bearings

Bows and crossbows

Part 2

Castles, forts and artillery, 8th to 15th century

Armour, 12th to 15th century

Infantry of the Renaissance

Cavalry of the Renaissance

The Slavs and Orientals to the end of the Renaissance

THE AGE OF CHIVALRY

PART 3
The Renaissance:
Arms, horses and tournaments;
Helmets and armour;
Tactics and artillery

Liliane and Fred Funcken

Prentice-Hall, Inc., Englewood Cliffs, N.J.

Contents

I WEAPONS, HORSES, AND TOURNAMENTS

Firearms

The arquebus

In Part 2 we saw how the crude 'gunpowder shaft' developed into something already bearing a strong resemblance to the arquebus, and unmistakably foreshadowing the modern rifle in shape.

The name 'arquebus' comes from the Italian *archibuso*, a corruption of the Dutch term *hakebusse*, which is in turn derived from the German *Hakenbüchse*, meaning 'hook-gun'. The hook referred to is, of course, the attachment beneath the barrel which could be hooked over a support or, quite simply, the merlon of a fortress parapet in order to absorb the powerful recoil of the weapon (see Part 2). Some of the more reputable writers on the subject interpret the term *Haken* more broadly to mean the serpentine (match-holder) or even the butt of the weapon, both of which were shaped like a hook. It should be pointed out, however, that the original 'harquebusses' did not have this curved butt. Similarly, in our opinion, the term *Doppelhaken*, meaning a type of heavy rampart arquebus, does not refer to the double serpentine but to the double calibre of this much larger weapon.

In England the arquebus was variously called 'hagbuse', 'hackbushe', 'harkbutte', and 'hagbut' – note here the gradual alteration of 'hack', and the adoption of 'but' or 'butte' in place of the original *Büchse*. Now in modern English 'butt' has several meanings, for example end, tree-trunk, rifle butt, or a blow from a horn, while 'hag' means witch or old fairy. Is it perhaps going too far to imagine the English in the early 16th century associating the new weapon with a kind of evil magic[1] – for evil it certainly turned out to be.

---

[1] We hope that our friends, the British and Irish experts W. Carman, A. Mollo, and G. Thompson, will forgive us this rash but attractive semantic hypothesis.

The popularity of this terrible weapon (it was described as 'accursed' in its day) grew despite the protests of noble knights who now found themselves liable to be shot down by the first commoner who came along. Even the Chevalier Bayard, that most gallant of knights, ordered every arquebusier who was taken prisoner to be hanged. Ironically enough, the great soldier was to die on 30 April, 1524, from an arquebus ball that broke his back.

The arquebus-à-croc, or ordinary 'haquebuse' or 'hackbut', still weighed as much as 20 to 30 kilos at the beginning of the 16th century. Earlier on, however, a lighter weapon appeared that could be

THE PISTOL
1. Matchlock pistol (*c.*1460). 2. Pistol with two superimposed charges (*c.*1560). The ball-shaped pommel could be opened out. It was used for holding spare pieces of pyrites. 3. Unusual right-angled German model (*c.*1550). The ball-shaped pommels are often thought to have been used as clubs, but in most cases they are too light to have been used for inflicting a blow. 4. Combined powder-horn and spanner (*c.*1550). 5. Italian pistol (1590). 6. Spanish pistol with a bar-type spanner (*c.*1550). This removed the risk of losing the key for tightening the spring of the wheel-lock (see the mechanism on the following plate). 6a. Spanner fitting inside the butt of the pistol (1550). 7. German miniature pistol measuring 5 cm in length. Despite its tiny size it could fire a bullet 2 mm in diameter. The same shape of grip was found on full-sized models, as in fig. 7a (1570). 8. German pistol (1591). 9. French pistol measuring 58 cm long (1580). 10. So-called 'Milanese' type of pistol (1580).

11. Pistoleer armed with four pistols (*c.*1580). His fire-power was far greater than that of an ordinary cavalryman, and this was thought to give him an important tactical advantage. The 'pistoyer' in the illustration is wearing a mail cape known as a 'bishop's mantle'. This garment was very popular in Germany in the 16th century.

Arming pistols rarely had any decoration on them, obviously in the interests of economy. This lack of ornamentation has led to their virtually total disappearance. Large numbers of de luxe models, on the other hand, have survived to the present day.

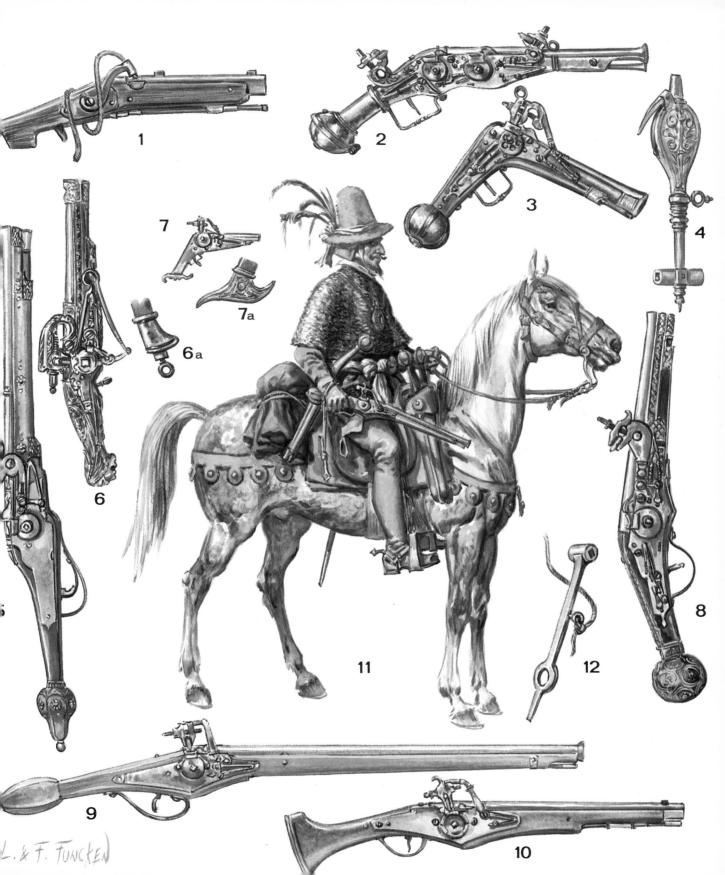

1

2

3

4

7

7a

6a

6

8

9

10

11

12

L. & F. FUNCKEN

raised to the shoulder and fired by one man. In Germany, too, an arquebus with a matchlock, pan-cover, and spring-operated trigger had been manufactured along industrial lines since 1475. Around 1510 the final improvement was made to the weapon, a 'fireguard'[1] that protected the eyes from sparks caused by the priming powder igniting suddenly in the pan. Henceforth the arquebus was to be used to equip infantrymen up until 1700, at any rate in less prosperous countries.

The matchlock

The design of the matchlock was absolutely straightforward and can be easily understood from illustrations. The mechanism consisted of a serpentine holding a slow-burning match that had to be 'compassed', or adjusted, until it exactly touched the priming-pan next to the sight on the barrel, thereby igniting the main charge.

Balls were made first of stone, and then of lead, and were kept in a small bag. The normal practice, however, was to keep two to four balls in the mouth while firing so as to save time when re-loading. This practice was so common that troops who surrendered with honours of war were granted the privilege of marching past with bullets in their mouths.[2] A flask of fine priming powder, a larger flask for charge powder and 2 to 3 metres of spare 'match' completed the arquebusier's equipment, or *fourniment*. This fairly elaborate equipment (called 'Dutch equipment') was to remain in use until the early 16th century.

In order to simplify the firing procedure little wooden[3] cases were devised, each of which contained a prepared charge, sometimes with a bullet in it. People tend to think that these strings of charges were only introduced in the early 17th century, but in fact they are much older. The bold and highly detailed German engravings from the first decades of the 16th century clearly show them being worn by landsknecht arquebusiers.

[1] Or 'flame-guard'. In Old English it was written 'fyre-garde' or 'fyreshielde'.
[2] A custom still practised in 1750.
[3] Wood was preferred to tin or copper, as these materials made too much noise and did not keep the powder as 'fresh'.

In addition there is a painting by Melchior Felsen which shows arquebusiers of the Holy Roman Empire using arquebusses ranging from the most basic model, without a serpentine, to the very latest version, complete with wheel-lock. Evidently, for reasons of economy, obsolete weapons went on being used until they wore out completely; in fact they probably continued to be manufactured because they were so cheap in relation to the latest 'novelties'.

LOCKS (1)
1. Matchlock hackbut (second half of the 15th century). It was also called an arquebus-à-croc as a wallpiece. The 'hook' projection served to lessen the gun's recoil when placed either over a rampart or in the trestle used to support the gun during firing. 2. Matchlock arquebus (c.1500). The trigger is shaped like a small knob (a). 3. Matchlock arquebus (c.1580). Length: 1.36 metres. 4. Matchlock musket (c.1590). Length: 1.78 metres. Because of its weight (10 kilos) a fork rest had to be used during firing: a) stock or butt; b) lock-plate; c) trigger, known as a key or spring. 5. Matchlock arquebus with a ten-shot cylinder (c.1530). A similar mechanism was used in pistols, though of course it was operated manually. 6 and 7. Matchlock breech-loading arquebus (c.1540). 8. Wheel-lock musket (16th century). It has a double trigger for precision shooting. 9. Early 16th century *Mönchsbüchse* (literally, monk's arquebus). This extremely simple weapon tends to be drawn with absurdly exaggerated proportions. Its actual length was in fact 29 cm, and it had a calibre of 1.2 cm. Its rasp (a) makes it the forerunner of the wheel-lock; it was activated by pulling on a ring (b). The other ring (c) was used to sight the weapon. (d) is the belt-hook for hanging it by. 10. Wheel-lock carbine (late 16th century). 11. Small wheel-lock arquebus (c.1600). This was a German-Polish model known as a *Tchinke*. Its external mechanism made it easier to maintain but it was vulnerable to knocks. 12. Inside and outside views of a match-lock showing the flame-guard (a) to protect the eyes from sparks shooting up from the priming-powder (late 16th century). 13. Inside view showing wheel-lock in firing position; the outside view shows it in loaded position.

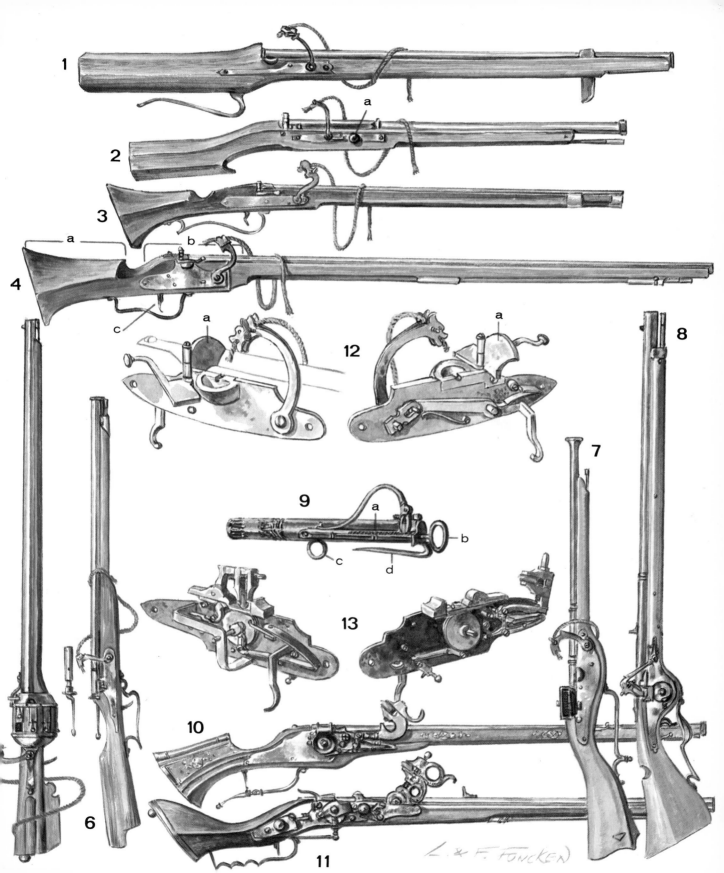

The wheel-lock

Between 1515 and 1520 the enterprising German armourers of Nuremberg made another vital step forward in the development of an effective firing mechanism. This was the wheel-lock, which worked by the friction of a wheel striking a piece of pyrites.[1] The original idea was put forward by Leonardo da Vinci between 1480 and 1485. Previous to that, an unknown scientist had already exploited the properties of pyrites in the early 15th century with the invention of the *Mönchsbüchse* (monk's arquebus), which is shown in the illustrations.

The wheel-lock mechanism used a wheel with a serrated edge attached to a spring and short connecting chain that could be wound up by a quarter turn of a key. To fire the weapon the hammer, with its piece of pyrites, was lowered over the pan-cover. When the trigger was pressed it moved aside the lid of the pan and simultaneously activated the spinning movement of the wheel. The serrated edge of the wheel struck the sparks needed to ignite the powder. Flint could be used in place of pyrites but it wore down the serrated edge of the wheel too rapidly. Pyrites, on the other hand, was very friable and left behind heavy deposits which clogged up the delicate mechanism so that it needed constant care and maintenance.

This type of lock was probably very expensive to buy. According to our calculations, a very ordinary wheel-lock arquebus must have cost at least 1500 pre-revaluation francs in 1580, whereas a matchlock arquebus would have cost only 350 to 400 francs.

In addition to the high purchase price there was the problem of the rather dicey 'after-sales service' – sending a weapon to Nuremberg or Milan must have been a very risky business in those troubled times. Germany, which did not suffer from these problems, began using the wheel-lock very late on, even after the invention of the flintlock system, and then only for hunting weapons.

---

[1] Yellow pyrites or cubic pyrites is an iron bisulphate that is found in the form of cubic crystals. It looks like metal and when polished can take on an attractive shine very similar to gold in appearance. It used to be called iron pyrites or arquebus stone.

The snaphance

The snaphance (the word is a corruption of the German *Schnapphahn*, meaning 'cock that pecks') first appeared in Germany in the second half of the 16th century and in Holland in 1530. From there it travelled to England, where it was used to arm the troops sent to fight in Ireland in 1580.

The snaphance worked by means of a piece of pyrites striking against a grooved steel plate or battery. Flint very soon took the place of pyrites, thereby making the snaphance the last stage but one in the development of the modern flintlock. Its use spread throughout Europe thanks to its relatively low cost (25% cheaper than the wheel-lock), its durability, and the simplicity of its mechanism.

LOCKS (II)

1. Twin-lock musket combining the matchlock and snaphance (mid-16th century). 2. Arquebusier's shoulder-belt with protective flap. Each tube contained enough powder for one shot. The bullets were kept in the small bag. A special flask was used to hold priming powder. 3. Arquebusier's shoulder-belt with his 'twelve apostles', or cartridges. The number of cartridges varied from less than twelve to as many as fifteen. Below (a), is an open cartridge. 4. German pistol with an external firing mechanism of the snaphance type (1580). This system was never to oust the wheel-lock in Germany. 5. Scottish pistol with a Dutch snaphance (early 17th century). 6. Blunderbuss with a miquelet lock (late 16th century). 7. Miquelet pistol (early 17th century).

8. Inside and outside views of an Italian snaphance lock (*c.*1600). 9. Scottish snaphance lock. 10. Dutch snaphance lock with its characteristic priming-pan button. 11. Spanish, or so-called 'miquelet' lock, invented *c.*1587. The miquelet lock marks the last stage before the final development of the famous flintlock. This system, which was introduced in 1630, was eventually adopted throughout the whole of Europe and was eventually used by every nation in Europe until after the wars of the first Empire (see *Arms and Uniforms – The Lace Wars*, Part I, p. 19). The term 'miquelet' was adopted in France in the mid-17th century; at this period the Spanish lock was being used by the 'Miquelets' – soldiers from Aragon and Catalonia.

12. Musketeer's combined fork rest and sword with a wheel-lock pistol attached (late 16th century). 13. Musketeer's combined fork rest and sword (late 16th century).

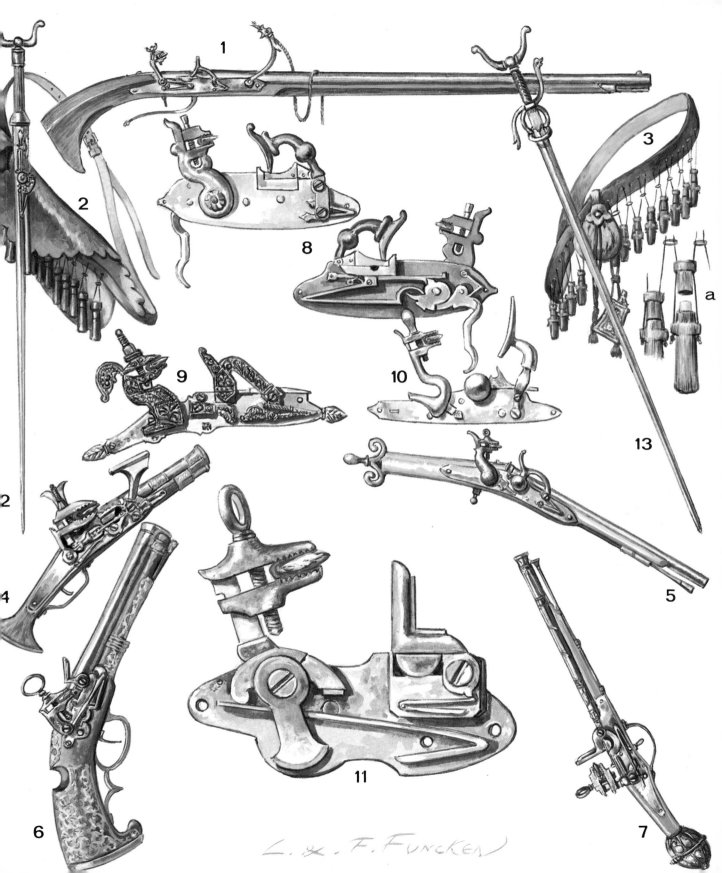

1

2

3

a

8

9

10

13

2

4

5

6

11

7

L. & F. FUNCKEN

The miquelet[1]

The last stage of development before the introduction of the flintlock proper was the miquelet, which was invented about 1584. At the time it was called the 'Spanish lock', as its inventor, Marquarte, worked in Spain, although he was a member of the Markhardt family of Augsburg.

The general apathy that greeted this revolutionary new system is quite staggering – after all, it was just a hairsbreadth away from the method that was to dominate European weapons from the 17th to the 19th centuries.

The musket

The musket was a large-calibre arquebus,[2] sometimes twice the weight and calibre of an ordinary arquebus, that was first used by the Spaniards in 1567. It took its name either from the Italian word *moschetto* (formerly a kind of sparrowhawk[3]) or the Spanish *mosca* (meaning sparks), but its etymology remains doubtful. One thing that is certain, however, is that it caused a sensation on account of its terrifying armour-piercing capacity.[4]

Because of its weight it had to be supported with a forked rest while in the aim position. However, as more and more armour was gradually discarded the musket became lighter; this in turn made the arquebus redundant, and from that time on, the term 'musket' was the only one to be retained.[5]

France was the slowest of all the European nations to adopt the arquebus and the musket.

At the beginning of his reign Francis I still preferred to use crossbowmen. About 1534 he introduced twenty per cent of 'hackbuteers' (heavy arquebusiers) and 'haquebusiers' (ordinary arquebusiers) into his legions. In 1552 arquebusiers made up thirty per cent of Henri II's troops. In 1572 Charles IX introduced the musket into his army, despite some misgivings. In 1580 the weight of a musket ball was still 31.35 grams while an arquebus fired a ball of 10.18 grams. Nevertheless in 1590 Henry II adopted the powerful 'Walloon-style' musket and equipped half of his forces with it.

The pistol

It seems that one or two examples of the matchlock pistol were invented as early as 1460; however, the wheel-lock version made its first appearance in Germany around 1517 and in Italy around 1521.

It was the reiters who were responsible for making the pistol widely known. The name pistol comes either from Pistoia, the home town of its inventor, Camelio Vetelli, or from the gold Spanish coin known as a pistola.[6] Another, more plausible,

[1] The name is explained in the caption to fig. 11, p. 53.

[2] The musket fired a ball weighing around 60 grams while the weight of an arquebus ball was 30 grams.

[3] This bird was called *moschet* or *mouchet* in Old French, and *émouchet* in modern French. 'It is well-known how common a practice it is to give names of animals to weapons, for example falconets and culverins' (Littré).

[4] From 1520 onwards a lighter type of rampart musket was adopted in Spain. It demonstrated its effectiveness at the siege of Pavia in 1524, where its 60-gram balls pierced even the thickest armour. This gun was already a musket in everything but name.

[5] In 1600 the arquebus weighed 5 kilos and the musket 8. An arquebus ball weighed 25 grams while a musket ball was around 50 grams.

[6] Similarly a short small pistol was called a tercerole, after the name of an Italian coin, the *terzarolo*.

ARQUEBUSIERS AND MUSKETEERS IN THE EARLY 17TH CENTURY

1. Arquebusier pouring priming-powder into the pan. At this period arquebusiers were the only soldiers to wear a helmet of some description. Musketeers wore a light hat in preference, because of the weight of their equipment. 2. Arquebusier waiting for the order to shoulder his weapon. He is covering the pan with his two fingers to prevent the 'match', placed in position in the serpentine, from causing the powder to ignite prematurely. The priming powder, charge, and bullets were carried separately along with the equipment known as a 'Dutch fourniment'. 3. Musketeer 'taking up his fork' in order to place his weapon in it after loading. Figs. 3, 4 and 5 show the bandolier with the charges ready for firing dangling from it. The small flask shown in the illustrations was only used for priming the pan. 4. Musketeer on the march. The fork was held like a walking-stick. 5. A trained musketeer was able to balance his loaded weapon in the fork using only the left hand.

1

2

3

5

4

L.XF. Fonoken

theory is that the name is derived from the Italian word *pistallo*, meaning the pommel of the saddle which the pistol was hung from before it was placed in holsters. In England the term 'dag' or 'dagge' was used; this was a contraction of 'demi-hagbutt' (meaning 'half-arquebus').

When the snaphance version of the pistol was invented its greater reliability led to its immediately superseding the wheel-lock[1] model.

Rifled weapons

The first rifled weapons appeared during the second half of the 15th century, almost certainly in Germany. The Austrian Gaspard Kollner gave a demonstration of rifling in Leipzig in 1498. Arquebusses have been found dating from 1460 that have eight, ten, or even more riflings running parallel to the length of the barrel. Shortly after this, Augustus Cotter of Nuremberg invented spiral rifling.

It is quite amusing to note that Cotter's successors, or rather imitators, completely failed to grasp the significance of his discovery, which was to prove so crucial to the development of ballistics. They exercised their imaginations greatly in devising new types of rifling, with what feeble results we might imagine. Fortunately, by 1530 more enlightened armourers had taken up Cotter's idea and continued to develop it. However as rifled weapons were prohibitively expensive to buy and slow to load[2] they were only used in battle on rare occasions before 1630.

Staff weapons

The halberd

Perhaps it is because of the harmless appearance of our church vergers,[3] but the fact is that the word halberd tends to conjure up visions of a fake weapon being carried around by some bit player in *Hamlet*. This *Helmbarte*, or handled axe (from *Helm*, a handle, and *Barte* or *Parte*, an axe) was a direct descendant of the voulge, which in turn evolved from the long-handled axe carried by 11th-century warriors.

Some writers have claimed that the halberd was imported into Denmark from China during the 15th century. From there it was supposed to have been brought to Germany, and then to Switzerland, where the Confederacy armies introduced it into France and it was used in Louis XI's armies. However, a mere glance at our table of staff-weapons in Part I proves that the halberd did not have to rely on the military genius of the Chinese to follow its logical development: thus, between the early 15th and the mid-16th centuries, it acquired a shape that was perfectly adapted to its murderous purpose.

By this time the halberd had been supplanted by the arquebus and had already begun to lose the characteristic features of a close-combat weapon. As its axe-head dwindled in size it lost some of its cutting power; then, during the second half of the

STAFF WEAPONS (I)
1. Diagram showing the various parts of the head of the halberd (the drawing is based on an early 16th century halberd): a) spike; b) die-mark; c) blade or axe-head; d) fluke; e) heel; f) socket; g) langets.

2. Swiss halberdier with standard-bearer of the canton of Uri (the standard represents the head of a black bull with a red ring through its nostrils). The helmet which the halberdier has hanging from his belt is a superb Italian sallet dating from c.1470.

3–5. First half of the 16th century. 6–9. Mid-16th century. 10. Second half of the 16th century. 11 and 12. Mid-16th century. 13. Second half of the 16th century. 14. Mid-16th century.

---

[1] The pistol could also fire bolts and short steel darts. Men-at-arms wearing armour would fire at point-blank range, holding their weapon literally against their opponent's cuirass.
[2] With rifled weapons a metal rod and a hammer had to be used to drive the bullet down inside the barrel.
[3] Translator's note: In France the verger, or *suisse*, wears a uniform based on that originally worn by Swiss mercenaries.

16th century, its tip grew disproportionately long until it took on the slender shape of an estoc. All the time that these changes were taking place (changes that were the direct result of the new fighting methods employed by the infantry and cavalry) the traditional version of the halberd continued in existence, albeit after a fashion. This model retained most of the old characteristic features, and it is the one we are most familiar with today: the various indentations on its axe-head are more decorative than functional. It was used to arm royal body-guards of the day and only ended its long career in the 17th century, as an elaborately decorated ceremonial weapon.

The pike

After a long absence from the stage of military history the long pike once carried by Greek soldiers was revived by the Swiss. In the process, medieval strategy in the 16th century was completely disrupted, as the chapter on the Swiss Confederacy shows. The pike was a very simple weapon consisting of a shaft (usually made of ash) with a splint or socket head; the metal arms, or langets, holding on the head varied in length and were fixed to the shaft by means of screws or rivets. The head was either shaped like a sage leaf or could have a more or less tapering triangular or square section; the latter shape was particularly effective against heavy armour.

The tremendously long shaft of the Swiss pike enabled soldiers standing in the fourth rank to reach at least 2 metres beyond their comrades in the front line. These four ranks, bristling with pikes, presented an impassable obstacle for knights on horseback. Ranks standing further back held their pikes upright in readiness to cover any breach made in the ranks.

Before the pike eventually disappeared from the battlefield it grew considerably in length, at times measuring 8 metres. This gigantic size served no useful purpose, however, except possibly to give

some consolation to raw recruits in the infantry ranks.

The firearm was responsible for the decline of the pike – and, indeed, the decline of all the other staff weapons. For a long time pikemen outnumbered the rest of the army, but from the mid-16th century onwards their strength in the battalions began steadily decreasing, until by the end of the century they were reduced to a third of the infantry.

An attempt was made to substitute a new type of pikeman clad in corselet armour for both the cuirassed double-pay front-line soldiers and the *picques seiches* ('dry pikes') on ordinary pay who made up the rest of the pike strength. However, the power of the firearm and the extra troops required, plus the exorbitant cost of equipping all the pikemen with armour, simply led to an increase in the number of poor-quality cuirasses. These were virtually useless to the pikemen wearing them, and they were got rid of at the first available opportunity.[1]

The partisan

Alongside the halberd and the pike there evolved a wide variety of short weapons, ranging from the

[1] It is worth pointing out that a kind of tacit agreement existed by which musketeers always fought other musketeers, and pikemen always attacked other pikemen (their pikes could only pierce armour with some difficulty). This was a curious survival of old traditions among 'professionals'.

STAFF WEAPONS (II)
1–6. Second half of the 16th century. 7 and 8. Early 17th century. 9. Partisan (late 16th century). 10. Wavy partisan (early 17th century). 11. 16th-century fouchard. This is called a *falcione* in Italian. 12. 16th-century brindestoc or brandistoc with an axe-head and a bec-de-corbin (crow's beak). This is the Italian version of the brindestoc, known as a *brandistocco*. 13. Brindestoc with spikes (16th century). This type of weapon had a long concealed blade that shot out from the hollow handle as a result of the centrifugal force exerted by a sharp half-turn of the wrist. It was particularly common in France and Italy. 14. Military fork, also called a 'harpin' (early 17th century).

15. Venetian arquebusier using a brindestoc-type fork with a retractable blade (early 16th century). 16. German halberdier (early 16th century).

1

2

6

5

3

4

7

9

10

15

16

8

11

12

13

14

L & F FUNKEN

épieu to the elegantly-shaped partisan. The ever-inventive and productive Italians produced a whole host of weapons with heads that were impressive to look at, if not exactly effective; examples of these are the corseque (see Part I, p. 80) and the new-style voulge and guisarme, both of which were decorated with superb engraving. These heavier, de luxe blades were all used in the myriad small courts of Germany; however, it was the pertuisane or partisan[1] that predominated. It existed in a whole range of styles, from the purely functional design, at one end of the scale, to the superb examples of goldsmiths' work owned by great leaders or the bodyguards of wealthy lords at the other.

The partisan continued to be used in many European courts up until the 18th century, and was also carried as a ceremonial weapon by officers and sergeants.

The bow and the crossbow

By the beginning of the 16th century the bow and the crossbow[2] (or arbalest) had both been made redundant by the advent of gunpowder. However, the bow, although an anachronism, did reappear from time to time, not without some degree of success. Hence it was used by Moors at the siege of Algiers in 1541 and by the English outside Boulogne in 1549.

The lance as a staff weapon

The knightly lance (already mentioned in Part I) was for a long time the ideal weapon for use in charges against the infantry or in single combat against an opposing knight.

Up until the 14th century the lance measured 3 to 4 metres in length. However, as fighting men took more and more to wearing armour for protection,

heavier and heavier lances were introduced, with heads of greater armour-piercing capability. The lance increased in length slightly, reaching 4 to 5 metres[3] after the 15th century. Evidently the weapons used in 'battles' varied considerably in width and length from one country to another.

The English were the first to shorten their lances and make their knights fight on foot (during the Hundred Years' War, in point of fact). The French and the Austrians occasionally followed their example (the latter, as we saw, at the battle of Sempach[4]).

Thus, according to Froissart, the lance was 'cut back to a length of 5 feet (à la mesure de cinq pieds)'[5]. This measurement seems to us to have given rise to some misunderstanding, as certain writers have taken it to mean that the length of lance remaining after shortening was 5 feet – the size of an *épieu*. We tend to feel that the 5 feet mentioned by Froissart refers to the amount *cut off* the length of the lance. Thus a weapon originally 13 feet long would have been reduced to a 'tool' of approximately $7\frac{1}{2}$ feet – which seems far more likely.

THE LANCE AND THE CUIRASS REST
A. Lance heads: 1–3. 12th century. 4 and 5. 1250. 6 and 7. 1270. 8 and 9. 1350. 10. Late 14th century. These heads are all drawn to scale and measure between 7 and 36 cm.

B. Cuirass rests: 1. Brooch-type (1350). 2. 1415. 3. Simple hook-shaped rest (1425). 4. 1440. 5. 1450. 6–8. 1480. 9. 1490. This rest has an inset of soft wood (lead was also used) to act as a 'shock absorber'. The teeth of the graper would bite into this (see the lance in fig. C1; the graper is shown at (a). 10 and 11. 1500. 12 and 13. 1510. 14. 1540. 15. 1550. 16. 1560. 17. 1570. 18. 1590.

C. Lances: 1. Lance with graper (a). It is 5 metres long (late 14th century). 2 and 3. 1300. 4. 15th century. 5. Late 15th century. 6 and 7. 1510. 8. 1520. 9–11. 16th century. 12. Early 16th century. Its length is 3.40 metres.

[1] The name 'pertuisane' comes from *pertuis*, meaning an opening – a reference to the gaping wounds inflicted by the weapon; an alternative and simpler derivation is from 'partisan'.

[2] See Part I, chapter III.

[3] The weapons carried by lancers just before they passed into obsolescence were sometimes 7 metres long – yet another example of the weapon becoming bigger as the soldier becomes less effective!

[4] See the chapter on the Swiss infantry, Part 2.

[5] Translator's note: The ambiguity of Froissart's account is lost in translation. The phrase 'à la mesure de 5 pieds' could be interpreted as 'by 5 feet' or 'to 5 feet' in the original French.

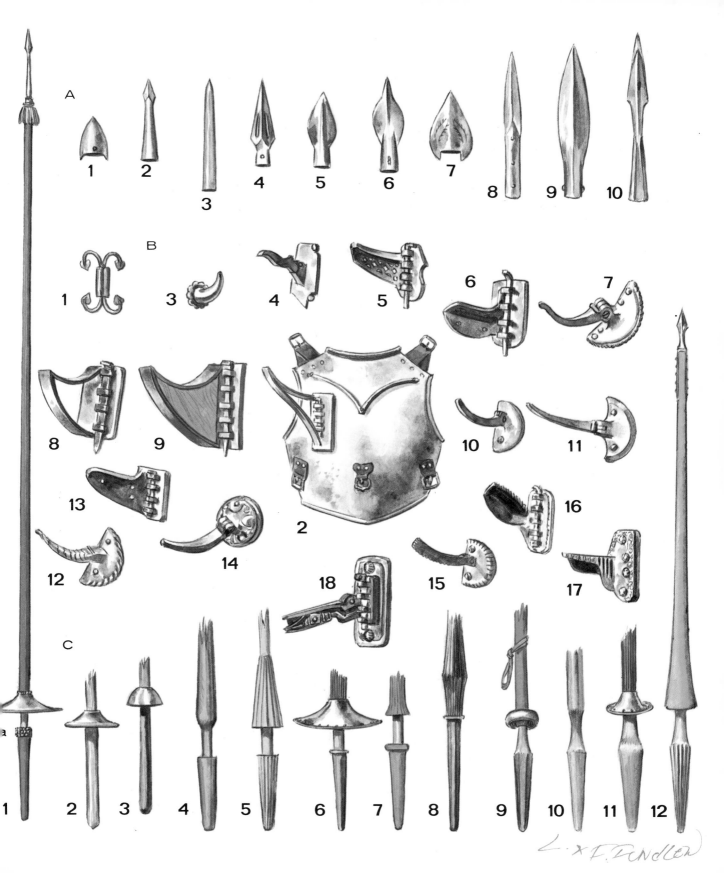

A

1 2 3 4 5 6 7 8 9 10

B

1 3 4 5 6 7

8 9 2 10 11

13 16

12 14 15 17

18

C

1 2 3 4 5 6 7 8 9 10 11 12

a

L.×F. Pendlow

The operation described as 'shortening' the lance, which was carried out during fighting, simply meant that the lance was held by the middle instead of by the butt. There was no question of anyone starting on a complicated last-minute carpentry job!

The cuirass rest

The cuirass rest, which is often mistakenly referred to as a faucre, or else tends to be confused with the lance rest, was a metal prong used to support the weight of the lance when it became too heavy to be held in the rest position by the man-at-arms. The rest also served to absorb the recoil following impact.

The lance rest

The lance rest started out as a simple leather strip on the handle of the lance that protected the hand from the shock of impact. The strip was next positioned behind the hand, following the introduction of the cuirass rest; it came down on the cuirass rest, and acted as a kind of buffer.

The leather strip gradually changed into a kind of collar called a 'grate' or 'graper', which was made of several rows of small balls or billets. In Spain and Italy a rondel with a serrated edge was used instead; the sharp points on it bit into the wood, cork, or lead covering that was found on the more solid type of cuirass rest.

The decline of the lance

We can tell the direction in which the lance developed, and its eventual fate, simply by looking at illustrations of cuirass rests. For the cuirass rest became an increasingly rare feature of suits of armour, and the original sturdy versions grew more and more spindly in shape. The latter rests were designed for a more fragile type of lance, wielded by men-at-arms who were gradually losing confidence in the effectiveness of their weapon as the growing strength of the infantry made it appear increasingly insignificant.

SWORDS AND DAGGERS (I), 9TH–13TH CENTURIES

Swords: 1–3. 9th century. 4 and 5. 10th century. 6–9. 11th century. Total length (fig. 9): 90 cm. 10. Second half of the 12th century. Total length: 95 cm. 11. 11th century. 12. 12th century. 13 and 14. Late 12th century. 15. First half of 13th century. 16. Second half of 13th century. 17. Mid-13th century. 18–20. Late 13th century. 21. Heavy horse sword (second half of 13th century). 22. Second half of 13th century. 23. Late 13th century.

24. Diagram showing the various parts of the sword: a) pommel; b) grip; c) guard or crossguard; d) tang; e) blade; f) tang-nut or button. The nut holding these various pieces together was made by riveting over the end of the tang.

Daggers: 25. 9th century. 26. 10th century. 27. 11th and 12th centuries. 28. 13th century. 29. Late 13th century; called a baselard (from Basel). This civil and military weapon was to evolve into the Swiss and German types of daggers after enjoying wide popularity throughout the 14th century. 30 and 31. 13th century.

FENCING IN THE 15TH AND 16TH CENTURIES (pp. 24–25)

Listed here are some typical fencing positions taken from manuals of the period: 1. With a sword. 2. With a rapier. 3. With a two-handed sword: *Seconde* position. 4. With a two-handed sword: *Prime* position. 5. With a dusack. 6. With a sword and a 'main gauche'. 7. With a braquemart.

Several of the contestants in the illustration are wearing *Hosenteufel* (devil's breeches) which people wore in defiance of all the preachers of the Reformation period. This exaggerated form of dress was especially popular in Germany.

8. Hand-and-a-half sword; also known as an estoc (first half of 16th century). The reinforcing piece at the base of the blade was called a quillon block. 9. Rapier (mid-16th century). 10. Two-handed sword; known as an espadon or flamberg (late 15th century). The term 'two-handed sword' was later used in the mid-17th century to mean a type of very long sharp sword. 11 and 12. Dusacks. 13. Braquemart (mid-17th century). It was also known as a 'malchus'.

14. Knights fighting with war hammers (early 15th century). This picture is taken from an illustration of the period by the artist John Rows. After the contestants had jousted and a lance had been broken they occasionally fought with war hammers or a thrusting lance (fig. A). The contest would end with a sword-fight (figs. B and C). The figure on the left in the picture is Richard Beauchamp, Count of Warwick, and his opponent is an Italian knight, Pandolfo Malatesta. Obviously contests like this were highly formalized and were fought according to a strict code of rules. The judge could stop the fight by throwing down his baton.

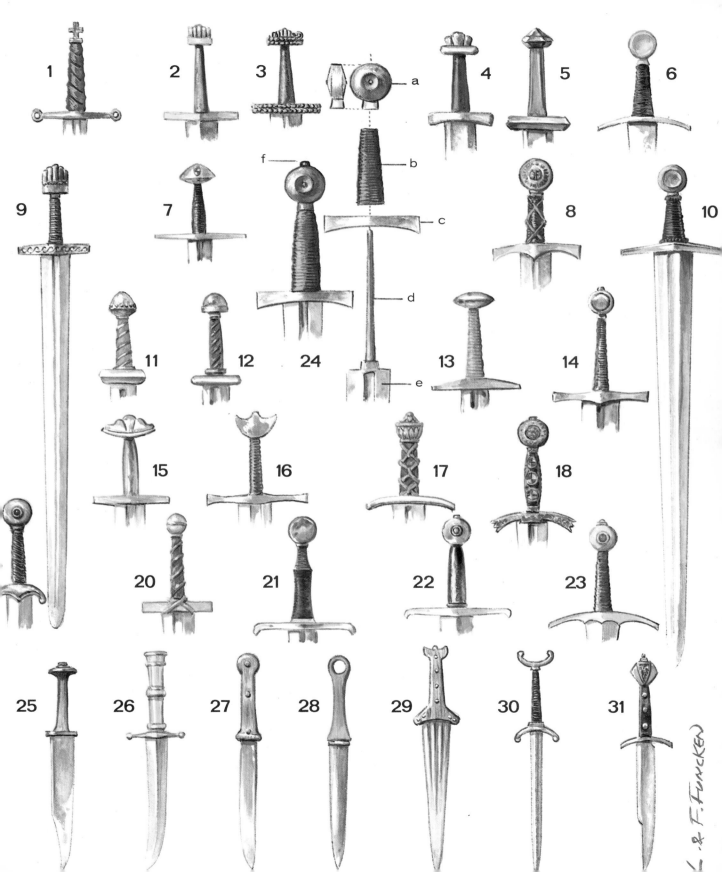

10

3

5

7

C

14

12

13

L. & F. FONCKEN

The sword

We never fail to be impressed by the spectacular swordplay of the swashbuckling heroes of film and TV dramas. What herculean strength it must have taken (we say to ourselves) to wield the heavy steel blades of the Middle Ages, which clanged like railway lines when they were struck together!

Let us not be under any illusions about this, however – the sword was, in fact, surprisingly light. We have attempted to find out the weight of a selection of swords from different periods, and our findings are that the average weight of swords from the 10th to the 15th centuries was 1.3 kg, while in the 16th century it was 0.9 kg.

Even the heavier bastard swords which were used only by second-grade fighting men did not exceed 1.6 kg, while the horse swords known as 'hand-and-a-half' swords weighed 1.8 kg on average. When due allowances are made, these surprisingly low figures also hold good for the enormous two-hand sword, which was traditionally only wielded by 'true Hercules'. Yet it seldom weighed more than 3 kg.

The development of the sword

The 9th-century sword was broad and relatively short, and had as its typical features a small hilt or cross-guard and a broad flat pommel, often shaped like a trefoil. In the 10th century the pommel acquired more of a rounded or tapering shape, while the hilt became more pronounced. As the large number of illustrations show, from the 15th century onwards the sword continued to grow increasingly slender in shape. The reader should refer here to the illustrations, which are far easier to understand than a long explanation.

The blade

The blade is the most important part of the sword, and it was made out of a very hard steel – so hard, in fact, that modern files make little impression on it. Famous centres of sword-making soon grew up,

[1] Toledo reached the height of its renown in the 16th and 17th centuries.

towns like Passau, Nuremberg and Augsburg, then later on Solingen with its trademark of a running wolf. Milan and Toledo,[1] in particular, attained a high level of craftsmanship, so much so in fact that certain armourers from Solingen did not hesitate to forge the stamp of Toledo on their products. There is no question that the Spanish master-craftsmen – like, for example, the Sahagun dynasty – were the main source of inspiration for the German and Italian swordmakers, whose original work has made deservedly famous names like Piccino, Horn and Tesche.

Paris and Brussels, along with many other towns, were responsible for producing top-quality sword

SWORDS AND DAGGERS (II) 14TH AND 15TH CENTURIES

Swords: 1–3. 1300. 4. Mid-14th century. 5. Second half of the 14th century. 6. Heavy arming sword (1380). This has a kind of cap to prevent any rain from entering the scabbard. 7. 1400. 8. Dress sword (1410). 9. 1410. 10 and 11. 1450. 12. Saddle sword (1450). Length: 1.25 metres. 13. Saddle sword that hung from the rider's saddle (mid-14th century). Length: 1.25 metres. 14. Cutting sword (late 14th century). Length: 95 cm. 15. Saddle sword (1450). Length: 1.5 metres. It has a false removable crossguard (a). 16. Heavy two-handed saddle sword (late 14th century). Length: 1.5 metres. 17 and 18. 1450. 19. Archer's or crossbowman's sword (1450). 20. Spanish sword (second half of 15th century). First appearance of the pas-d'âne (a). 21. Swiss sword (late 15th century). 22. Mid-15th century. 23. Dress sword (late 15th century). 24. Late 15th century. 25. Late 15th century. First appearance of the horizontal ring guard (a).

The swords in figs. 12, 13, 15 and 22 are the French ancestors of the *hegyestör* or pike-sword used by Hungarian hussars (see Part 2 of *Arms and Uniforms – The Lace Wars*).

Daggers: 26. Swiss dagger (late 14th century). It is descended from the baselard shown in fig. 29, p. 23. 27. Early 14th century. 28. Swiss dagger (mid-14th century). 29. Rondel dagger (mid-14th century). 30. Rondel dagger (early 14th century). 31. Early 14th century. 32. Rondel dagger (mid-15th century). 33. Late 15th century. 34. Ballock-knife or kidney dagger (14th century). 35. Ear dagger (15th century).

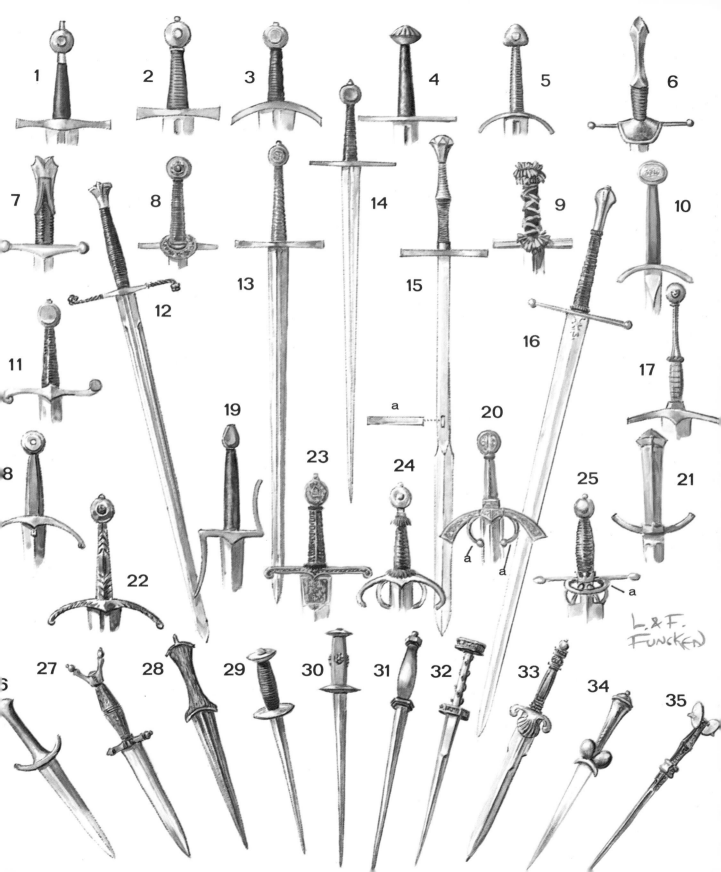

blades. However, as was the case with armour, they continually found themselves up against fierce competition from the three great German centres. We must not forget to mention the British, either, who began producing Sheffield steel as early as the 16th century.

The medieval knight was never without his sword; it was his inseparable companion, the noblest of weapons. The sword was sanctified by the Church, to whose service its owner dedicated himself. From the 9th century the sword-blade bore inscriptions, in many cases undecipherable, that were similar to those found on Viking weapons. Then, from about the 10th century, they began to carry Latin tags such as *In Nomine Domini* (in God's name) or *Homo Dei* (man of God). These, however, were probably felt to be too terse and they were replaced by longer phrases, abbreviated to a string of initials. Like most of the abbreviations that invade our daily lives, they were quite incomprehensible to the uninitiated. At the end of the 12th century changes were introduced that were designed to make the sword both a stabbing weapon and, at the same time, one capable of penetrating the increasingly heavy armour being made. These changes resulted in there being less surface area available for inscriptions. Even swords with a central reinforcing ridge down the middle no longer bore inscriptions, even though in some cases they had a flattened area near the hilt where a motto or invocation could be added.

The wide necks found on many swords were simply intended to lighten the weight of the weapon and not (as a silly but persistent legend has it) to 'help make the blood flow'.

A huge number of dress swords have come down to us intact, saved from destruction by their sheer beauty. These weapons rank, in fact, among the finest examples of the goldsmith's craft, and were decorated by the leading artists of the day – Dürer, Holbein and Cellini, to name only the most famous. Older swords, like the inscribed ones we have just mentioned, had to make do with a minimum of decoration – an engraved coat-of-arms, or some religious symbol, for example. As for the lettering, this was made by engraving sunken characters with a burin and inlaying them with fine wire, copper, or latten that was then hammered flat under heat.

Later on more elaborate motifs were used, which in some cases were inlaid with gold; hilts and pommels were made of solid gold and silver and decorated with pearls and precious stones. However we should beware of being taken in by the gorgeous appearance of some of the swords on display in our museums. Craftsmen of olden days were wonderfully skilled at cutting precious and semi-precious stones into fine wafers and producing emeralds and rubies which were entirely fake apart from the top layer. Thanks to this method many a vain gentleman was able to parade riches he did not in fact possess. At any rate we can be sure there was no shortage of takers.

The arming sword, which in any case was unsuitable for displaying such ornamentation because of its essentially practical function, had in the meantime grown increasingly narrow. Consequently the position of the unobtrusive emblems on it, including the armourer's stamp, was shifted so that they appeared either on the *ricasso* just below the hilt or, alternatively, on the escutcheon (both positions can be seen in the illustrations).

SWORDS IN THE 16TH CENTURY
1–3. Early 16th century. 4 and 5. Mid-16th century. 6. Franctaupin (mid-16th century). This may be the 'verdun' referred to in old manuscripts; it is without doubt the precursor of the 17th century colichemarde. 7–9. Early 16th century. 10 and 11. First half of the 16th century. 12. Sword-grip used in the mid-16th century. 13. Mid-16th century. 14. German arming estoc (mid-16th century). 15. Lansquenette (first quarter of 16th century); the so-called *Katzbalger* (literally, cat-gutter). 16. German arming estoc (mid-16th century). 17. Mid-16th century. 18. Hand-and-a-half or bastard sword (mid-16th century). 19. Spanish sword (mid-16th century). 20. Hand-and-a-half sword (c.1540). 21 and 22. 'Modified' two-hand sword (c.1560). 23. 1550. 24. 1560. 25. 1570. 26. 1580. 27. Bastard sword (second half of 16th century). 28. Spanish sword (c.1580). 29. Rapier (c.1570). 30. Spanish dress sword (c.1540).

The swords in figs. 13, 17 and 20, which all have basket hilts, are early versions of the classic schiavona shown in the following plate (fig. 11).

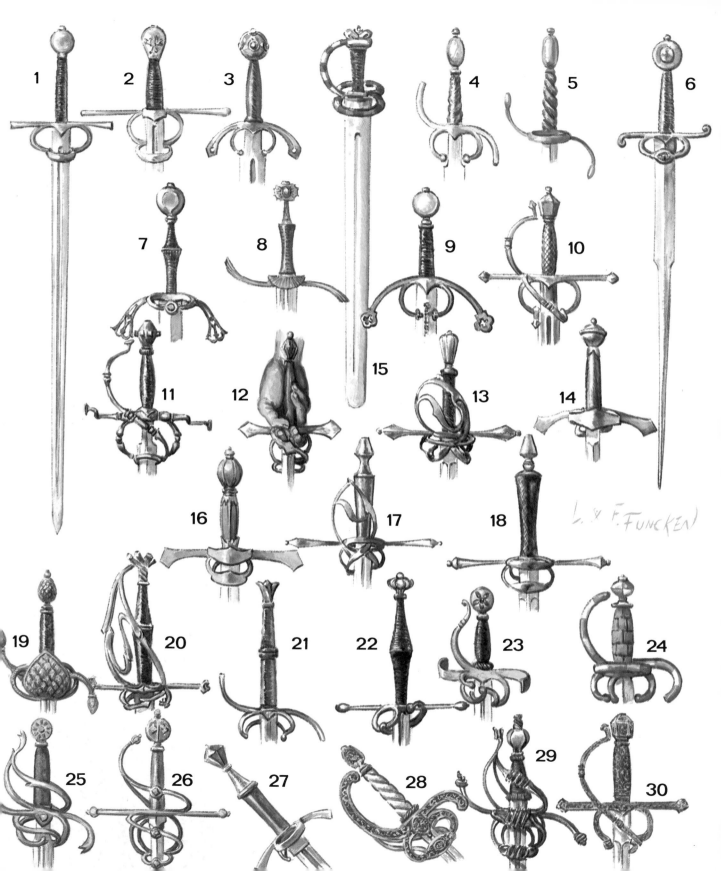

The poets of the Middle Ages have handed down to us the names of famous swords. Hence we know the names of Durendal, La Joyeuse, and Excalibur, which were owned by Roland, Charlemagne, and King Arthur respectively. Probably less well-known to us are Hauteclaire (belonging to Oliver), Basilarde (owned by Renaud), and Balmung (the sword of Siegfried). The Arabs, who were great lovers of epics, had little to learn from us in this area. Mohammed alone had nine sabres, each of which had its own name (Mabur, Daulfakar, Al Hatif, Al Rosub, etc). Mohammed's fourth successor and adopted son, Ali the 'Lion of God', was to make his sword Zolphagar the supreme emblem of the Islamic conquerors.

Terminology

The confusion on the subject of swords and edged weapons that tends to reign in dictionaries and even some specialist works has prompted us to attempt a more precise classification and definition of the terms used in these three volumes. We have drawn on the many works consulted by us in the course of our research to help produce the following short lexicon:

alenas: dagger with a rondel hilt and long sharp blade, triangular in section.

anlace: broad-bladed dagger, maximum length 50 cm.

arming sword: the classic battle sword, worn at the side.

badelaire, also called *baudelaire, bazelaire, basilaire:* type of scimitar with a slightly curved blade.

bastard: term most commonly used for a heavy sword with a long handle that could be grasped with both hands; also called a 'hand-and-a-half' sword. It has no connection with the big two-hand sword.

branc, also called *brand:* large horse sword; ancestor of the estoc.

braquemart: type of scimitar with a straight blade.

braquet: short sword with a slightly curving blade, used by the Walloons; forerunner of the *briquet.*

brette: another term for rapier.

cinquedea: cutlass belonging to the same family as the dagasse; also called *sang-de-dez.* It was five fingers broad at the heel.

claybeg: Scottish sword with a basket hilt, modelled on the Italian schiavona. It is now known as a *claymore.*

claymore: Scottish two-handed sword; often confused with the ordinary sword of the same period known as a *claybeg.*

SWORDS AND DAGGERS (III), 16TH AND EARLY 17TH CENTURIES
Swords: 1. *Circa* 1570. 2 and 3. 1575. 4. Short German sword (c.1585). 5–10. Late 16th century. 11. Venetian schiavona (late 16th century). 12. Early 17th century. 13. Sword with a spring-loaded dagger blade (late 16th century). 14. Rapier (mid-16th century). 15. Rapier (c.1600). 16. Late 16th century. 17. Flamberg (late 16th century). 18 and 19. Late 16th century. 20 and 21. Early 17th century. 22. Pair of rapiers for duel with two swords (late 16th century). The two weapons could be stored in the same scabbard; when in this position they fitted together and looked like a single sword.

23. Diagram showing parts of sword (second half of 16th century). Our model is an example of the work of the famous Piccinino of Milan, and was commonly called a *striscia*: a) tang-nut or button; b) pommel; c) grip; d) knuckle guard or bow; e) arm; f) crossguard front arm; g) crossguard back arm; h) escutcheon; i) pas-d'âne; j) counterguards; k) ricasso; l) inner horizontal ring guard; m) outer horizontal ring guard; n) groove. The Italians called the interlaced arms *gabbia* (a cage). Less elaborate models, like the one shown in fig. 21, were described as *mezza gabbia* (half-cage).

Daggers: 24. Anelace (c.1500); also called a cinquedea (literally, 'five fingers' broad), dagasse, sang-de-dez or san-de-dei; often mistakenly called a langue-de-boeuf. 25. Dagger called a *pistolese* in Italian (1500). 26. Mid-16th century. 27. Swiss dagger (mid-16th century). 28. Dagger with spring-loaded sword-breaker blades (mid-16th century); called a *sinistra* (literally, 'left'). 29. Misericorde (16th century). 30. Mid-16th century. 31 and 32. Late 16th century. 33. Sword-breaker (late 16th century). 34. Dagger (c.1610). It has a watch set in its pommel. Daggers with a shell shape protecting the hand at the hilt are often called 'mains gauches' or left-hand daggers. Spring-loaded models (fig. 28) looked rather terrifying but were less effective than the traditional dagger and were never really widely used.

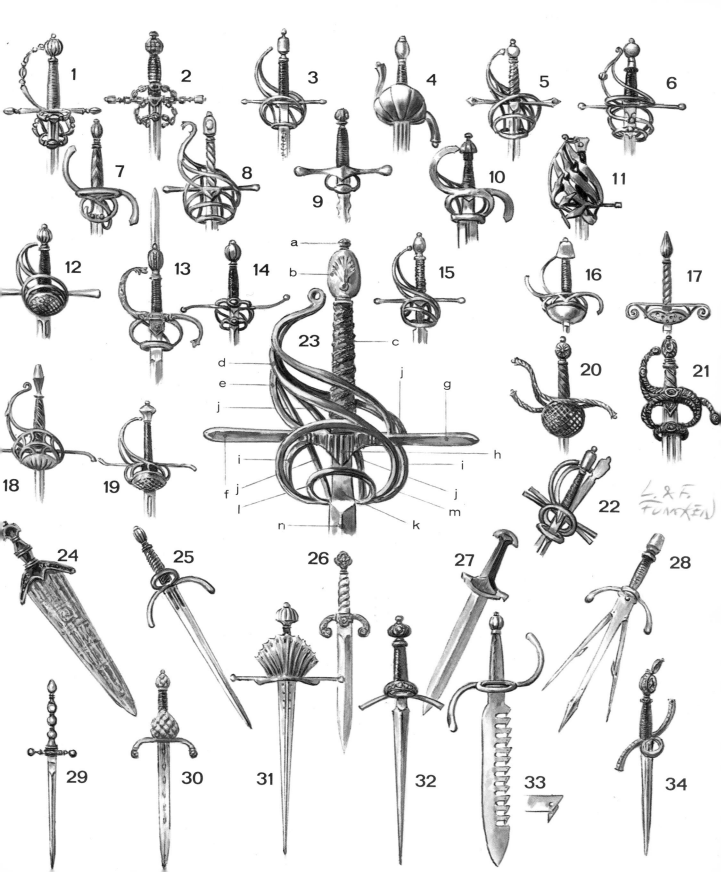

1 2 3 4 5 6
7 8 9 10 11
12 13 14 a b 15 16 17
23 c d e j j g 20 21
i h
i f j l n k m j 22 L. & F. FUNCKEN
24 25 26 27 28
29 30 31 32 33 34

colichemarde (a corruption of Königsmark, the name of its inventor): 17th century sword, broad at the heel and tapering abruptly towards the point.

coustil à croix: short sword with a blade that is very broad at the heel.

couteau à plates, de passe, taillant: heavy dagger with a broad heel.

coutille: bastard sword similar to the broad-heeled dagger.

cuirass-breaker: heavy dagger with a square section.

cutlass: another term for badelaire.

dagasse: large dagger related to the cinquedea.

Düsack: weapon of Bohemian origin, widely used by German peasants in the 16th century. Also called *Tesak* and *Messer* (knife).

esclavone: another term for schiavona (see below).

espadon: two-handed sword with a wavy blade; later used for any long broad sword. The term demi-espadon is used for a sword with a flat, straight blade.

estoc: large sword or horse sword; successor to the old branc. Often wielded by two hands for thrusting. This was the favourite weapon for single judicial combat.

estocade: term sometimes used for the heavy sword carried by lancers at the end of the 16th century.

falchion: another term for badelaire.

flambe, flambard, or *flammard:* medium-weight sword with wavy blade.

flamberg: popular name for long swords, especially two-handed swords with wavy blades. In England used to mean a rapier; later used only in a pejorative sense in France.

franc-taupin: sword with blade that tapered abruptly half-way along its length; similar to the coliche-marde.

glaive: short sword with a broad blade in the 16th century.

hegyestör: Hungarian version of the branc and the estoc; long sword designed to pierce armour and take the place of the lance.

lansquenette: short sword carried by the landsknechts.

mail-piercer: dagger with a square section.

malchus: type of badelaire. The name is a reference to the Biblical character whose ear was cut off by St Peter.

misericorde: sharp dagger for penetrating between the joins of cuirasses.

'passot' sword: very sharp sword carried by foot-soldiers.

'plate' sword: sharp sword designed for piercing early suits of armour.

pedarme: heavy sword carried by cuirassiers at the end of the 16th century. Square section.

prie-à-Dieu: another term for misericorde.

rapier: sword with a broad, sharp blade. The term *rapière* disappeared from French in the 15th century only to reappear in English and German in the form 'rapier'. From the 16th century onwards it was used only in a pejorative sense in France, like flamberg.

schiavona: heavy Venetian sword with a basket hilt; widely copied throughout Europe.

scimitar: oriental curved sword; from the Persian *chimchir* or *chimichir.*

stramazon or *stramaçon:* name given to swords of the Italian schiavona type or the Scottish claybeg type.

tuck or *tucke:* another term for rapier used in 16th-century England.

two-hand sword: big sword of Swiss or German origin; used by the Confederacy armies and the landsknechts.

verdun: type of very long, narrow sword made at Verdun; in use only as a duelling sword by the end of the 16th century.

HARNESS (I)
1. 8th century. 2. 9th century. 3. 11th century. 4. 12th century. 5. 1250. 6. 1260. 7. Mid-13th century. Mail trappers were very rare because of their high cost and they were often replaced by fabric reinforced at the neck and chest. 8. Late 14th century. 9. 1400.

10. Hungarian saddle (13th century). 11. Ivory saddle (late 15th century). 12. War saddle (early 15th century). 13. Ivory saddle (late 15th century).

Judicial duels and duels of honour

The judicial duel had met with fierce opposition ever since the reign of Charlemagne. It was condemned outright in the two canons issued by the Council of Valencia in 855 AD, but with the accession of Lothair in 954 AD, this horrible parody of justice grew more widespread. It lasted until the reign of Louis IX, in 1226, when the monarch succeeded in limiting this barbarous institution to disputed cases only. Unfortunately Louis X, who was a weak ruler, allowed it to re-establish itself in 1315. The incidence of these fights to the death became so high that some enterprising landowners had sites laid out that could be hired, ready for use, complete with fences and stands for the spectators.

Nobles always fought with noblemen's weapons, while villeins used the baton. Participants frequently wore special clothing that had been carefully oiled so as to leave their opponent the minimum of purchase – basically with the aim of prolonging the hideous display for as long as possible. The death of Jacques Legris, who was later acknowledged to be entirely innocent in a confession by the real culprit, provided a salutary shock, and judicial duels were abolished in 1385 by order of Charles VI.

Louis XII and Francis I agreed to the introduction of the duel of honour under pressure from the nobility. In this form of duelling the fight could be stopped whenever either of the combatants wished, by throwing a kind of sceptre into the lists.[1]

Prior to this, Charles VIII had personally presided over several 'official' duels of honour. Francis I was not averse to attending these occasions either, and his successor was present when La Châtaignerie was killed by Guy Chabot's[2] 'coup de Jarnac' (Jarnac's cut).[3] In desperation Henri II banned duelling altogether, but his subjects simply carried on without royal permission. Neither Charles IX's ordinance of 1566, nor the edicts of Henri IV and Louis XIV making duelling one of the major crimes, could prevent it from spreading like wildfire.

Duelling had its legendary figures, but it was not without its characters either. Take, for example, the lord of Gensac, who fought two opponents single-handed – simply to get a mention in the chronicles. Then there were cold-blooded killers like the Baron de Vitaux, whom Brantôme called the 'brave baron'. He fought at the side of his 'two lions', the Boucicault brothers, and the three of them would leave a trail of corpses in their wake. Louis de Clermont D'Amboise, known as the 'beau Bussy', who was immortalized by Alexandre Dumas in *La Dame de Monsoreau*, was little more than an incorrigible brawler. Among his many other misdeeds there was the time when he seized the opportunity offered by the St Bartholomew's Day Massacre to cut the throat of one of his relatives with whom he happened to be engaged in a lawsuit. He later died at the hands of hired killers employed by the husband of the fair damsel referred to earlier.

There were also group duels in which the favourites, or *mignons*, of Henri III and (surprisingly enough) the rugged Duke of Guise would battle it out together. Paradoxically, these effete young men fought with the energy and ferocity of wild beasts –

---

[1] A perfect example of the duel of honour can be found in the Chevalier Bayard's killing of the Spanish captain Soto-Mayor. Bayard had challenged him to a duel to obtain satisfaction for breach of promise and slanderous and untruthful remarks.

[2] Guy de Chabot, lord of Jarnac, had been insulted by the future King Henri II during a disagreement between the Duchess d'Etampes and Diane de Poitiers. As the prince could not fight in person, a champion had to be appointed in his place – a first-class fencer called La Châtaigneraie. When Henri became King he authorized the duel which his father had banned to go ahead; however in the interim Jarnac had been taking lessons from an Italian swordsman and had learned a new cut that made up for his relative lack of skill. In the course of the duel he severed his opponent's hamstring; La Châtaigneraie was too humiliated to seek medical help and died later from loss of blood. Jarnac was killed in a duel fifteen years later, in 1572.

[3] Translator's note: The fencing term 'coup de Jarnac' has also come to have the figurative meaning of 'a stab in the back' in modern French.

HARNESS (II)
1. 1390. 2. 1430. 3. 1450. 4. 1470. 5. 1500. 6. 1547. 7. 1550. 8. 1558. 9. 1580.

10. Ivory saddle (late 15th century). 11. War saddle (early 16th century). 12 and 13. Late 16th century saddles; three-quarter view of the back and front.

surely something for historians to reflect upon. The victims of such duels were buried in marble tombs in the form of a statue of the dead man. This custom gave rise to a new saying, so that a victor in a duel would say 'I've just carved him in marble' whenever an opponent had been successfully despatched. The duel that took place between the 'favourites' in 1578 was naturally enough followed by a duel between those favourites' favourites; this was fought between three pairs of fencers. When one of the duellists was killed, his two companions had to take on three opponents and both ended up by being run through. Encounters like this had precious little to do with honour.

In addition, fencing was a crudely unsophisticated sport at this period; every stroke and every trick in the book were permissible. The accounts of Brantôme, d'Aubigné, l'Estoile, and Tallemant clearly show that the majority of duels degenerated into murder. This passion for duelling is calculated to have cost the lives of 8,000 French gentlemen during the period between 1598 and 1608. Montaigne, who was born in 1533, wrote in his *Essays*: 'When I was a child, members of the nobility shunned a reputation as a good fencer; they slunk away out of sight to learn fencing, as they would an artful occupation unworthy of true and natural valour . . . We go to Italy in order to learn fencing and engage in it at the risk of our lives without knowing how to do it properly . . . If you put three Frenchmen in the deserts of Libya, they would not be together for a month before they began harassing and scratching away at one another'.

Henry IV issued an ordinance in 1599 officially banning duelling. Yet this did not stop him from fighting duels by proxy, for trifling reasons, or from giving out 7,000 letters of pardon to offenders. The duel of honour proper was only finally abolished in 1626 by order of Cardinal Richelieu, but clandestine duelling was carried on with renewed vigour. Louis XIV issued eleven successive edicts, but to no avail. Possibly one of the most tragic victims of this period was Armand de Sillègue, Lord of Athos, the famous character depicted in *The Three Musketeers*.

He was killed by a swordthrust on the Pré-aux-Clercs[1] on 21 December 1643. Unfortunately he would have had a difficult time going through all the adventures he experienced in *Twenty Years After!*

The judicial duel was known throughout the whole of Europe, but outside France the only country where ordinary duelling enjoyed any degree of popularity was Great Britain, and more especially Scotland and Ireland. Spain, Italy (particularly Naples), Austria and Germany all had difficulty in curbing the excesses of duelling, despite its being less prevalent in these countries. In Portugal there were only a very small number of duels fought.

Treatises on fencing

The first fencing manual that could be ranked on a par with the treatise on heraldry which was considered essential reading for every medieval gentleman appeared in Italy in 1410. It was entitled *Flos duellatorum* (or, in the vernacular, *Il Fior di Battaglia*), and was written by the 'maestro' Fiori dei Liberi. However, for a long time previous to this, travelling

[1] The Pré-aux-Clercs, in Paris, was the scene of countless duels. It was also the reason (and the setting) for the torture of Baptiste Crocoezon, the first 'ecologist' in France. He had waged an unsuccessful battle against the 'developers' of the early 16th century.

THE SPUR
1 and 2. 8th century. 3. 10th century. 4 and 5. Early 11th century. 6. Early 12th century. 7. Early 13th century. First appearance of the rowel. 8. Early 14th century. 9. 1350. 10. 1370. 11. 1400. 12. 1430. 13. 1400. 14. Early 15th century. 15. Second half of 14th century. 16. Late 14th century. 17. Early 15th century. 18. Mid-15th century. 19–22. Late 15th century. 23. Early 15th century. 24. Second half of 15th century. 25. Early 16th century. 26. Late 16th century. 27. Spur with a hollow stem and collar which could be used as a flask or for carrying secret messages (late 16th century). 28. Late 16th century. 29. Prickspur sewn in position on the foot-defences. 30. Late 14th century. 31. Diagram showing parts of spur: a) rowel; b) spindle; c) crest; d) stem; e) heelpieces; f) collars; g) strap-plate. 32. 1450. 33. Spur attached by the heelpiece (second half of 15th century.)

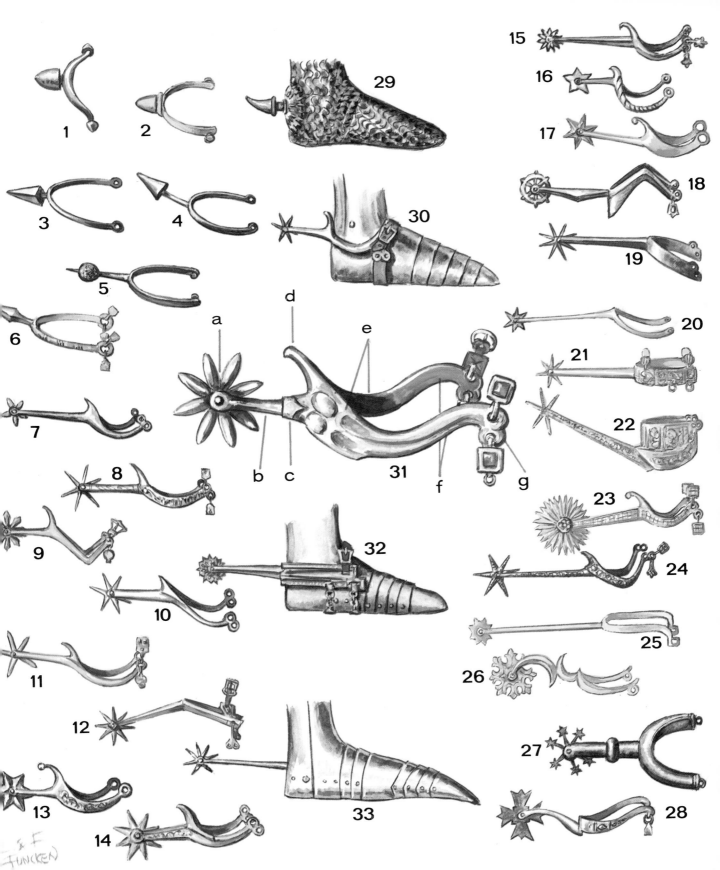

1

2

29

15

16

17

3

4

30

18

19

5

a

d

e

20

6

21

7

31

b   c   f   g

22

8

9

23

10

32

24

11

25

12

26

13

33

27

14

28

Σ F
FUNCKEN

fencing masters who were a cross between tumblers and rather shady hired men had been teaching their deadly skills in secret 'schools'.

In Germany it was the fencing masters who first opened the official *Fechtschulen*, or fencing schools, during the 14th century. From 1480 onwards these schools enjoyed various privileges and letters patent conferred by authority of the Emperor himself. The schools run by the Marxbrüder and the Feder-fechter[1] were the first to introduce swordplay using the new 'coup d'estoc' which was being popularized by the Italians Manciolino and Marozzo, and the Spaniard, Roman, at the beginning of the 16th century. Other Italians who came after them like Grassi, and Agrippa, the famous architect and mathematician, also wrote learned treatises; these were followed by works by the Frenchman Saint-Didier,[2] the Germans Lebkommer (with illust-rations modelled on Dürer) and Günterrod, and later by the Englishman, Silver.

These ancient manuals may seem ridiculous to present-day fencers but at the time they were bought up eagerly by all those in search of thrills and excitement. As manuals they must have been about as much practical use as the books published nowadays that claim to teach the reader how to become a millionaire in five lessons!

Forty thousand Frenchmen were killed in duels in the space of 180 years. That sobering statistic gives some idea of the disastrous effect these fighting manuals had on people. What was worse, they tended to be littered with pseudo-psychological and even theological observations. The book by Man-ciolino, published in 1543, contained far more dissertations on honour, and the different ways of challenging someone to a duel in a 'gentlemanly' manner, than information on the basic rudiments of fencing.

---

[1] *Feder* was a popular term for a rapier.
[2] The *Traicté contenant les secrets du premier livre sur l'espée seule, mère de toutes les armes* by St-Didier, was considered the first authentically French work on the subject of fencing. It is a compilation of the illustrations and methods used by the Italians Pagano, Grassi, and Agocchie, and goes some way to improving on Agrippa's book.

The horse

In the page or so devoted to the war horse in Part I we gave our personal opinion on the actual size of the 'great horse'. The subsequent research we have carried out has made us even more convinced that we were right in thinking that the war horse was not, in fact, bigger than average. The bards preserved in our leading museums today are displayed on models of horses made to fit the measurements of the armour, and they show just how averagely-sized the animals used in fact were. There is an obvious tendency towards exaggeration in the work of some early artists that has resulted in destriers being portrayed as massively big. Fortunately, however, the most celebrated painters and engravers of the day have left us a far more accurate artist's impres-sion. Dürer, Amman, Breugel, Titian and many others besides depict war horses that are no taller than 1.5 metres at the withers and yet are handsome-looking animals. We must not forget,

JOUSTS (I)
1. Heavy jousting in the German style with pointed lances. The reinforced armour they are wearing is of an extra-heavy type. The aim of the joust was to break the lance; blunt lances were often used as well. Note that the jousters in this plate have only to exert a minimum of effort to hold their lances in position because of the large cuirass rests on their armours. 2. German jousting of the *stechen* variety (*stechen*, to sting). Note the special backless saddle which allows the rider to leave the stirrups without breaking his back. The 'manteau d'armes' extending from the chin to the wrist was covered with leather so that lances could get a better purchase. Nevertheless, blunted lances are known to have been used as well, although they made for a less spectacular contest. Other plates in this volume show heavy armours designed for this form of jousting. It should be pointed out that although they protected the wearer from being injured by the lance, the sheer weight of them made them dangerous for the rider if he fell off his horse (see the place accompanying 'Jousts III').

1

2

either, the status of the famous sitters in several of these works. Would Francis I, Henri II, Maximilian, and Charles V have been prepared to see themselves portrayed on mounts whose size was not in keeping with their high rank?

Today the famous Lipizzaner horse of the equally renowned Spanish School in Vienna, which was originally bred on the stud-farms of Lipizza, near Trieste, measures 1.5 metres to 1.65 metres at the withers, given due care and attention. The original Lipizzaner horses were Andalusians, a breed already much sought after in the Middle Ages, which was descended from a remote cross between a 'pure German' horse, of the type brought over by the Vandals, and a barb or Barbary horse introduced from North Africa by the Arabs.

The Andalusian was subsequently to be used to help improve the stock of native breeds throughout Europe. William the Conqueror landed in England with two black half-bloods that had already evolved far beyond the heavy draught horses we might expect.

England and Germany both had an adequate supply of horses of the right build, but elsewhere the gendarmerie frequently had to make do with 'courtauds' while the light cavalry rode 'cavallins', or small light horses. As wars grew increasingly bloody so it became more difficult to obtain a steady supply of remounts, and most of the time the army had to make do with undersized mounts.[1]

In the early 16th century French heavy cavalry took up the bizarre practice of trimming the manes and ears of their mounts so they would look more frightening.

Bards

Since the beginning of the 15th century, horses had at times been quite literally barded in iron. All the skills of the beaters and furbishers went into making the finest examples of equestrian harnesses. It was the fashion at the time for de luxe suits of armour to come provided with matching bards, also lavishly decorated. Some armourers even submitted ideas for horse armour with jointed legs, but it is very

---

[1] An idea that people find it hard to associate with the French cavalry, and especially with the cuirassiers of the first Empire: the latter tend to be thought of as riding gigantic mounts.

doubtful whether these carefully worked-out schemes ever got beyond the planning stage.

In the mid-16th century the lack of protection these trappings afforded against the bullet led to them being gradually discarded; the only piece of defensive horse armour that was kept was the half-chanfron protecting the top half of the animal's head. Around 1580 this last remaining piece also disappeared from use. Its place was taken by a 'muserol' of forged metal openwork similar to a muzzle. By the end of the 16th century this piece had been adopted by the whole of the German cavalry.

In the meantime, at the beginning of the century, leather bards had been introduced in Italy; these, however, were soon to be replaced by leather straps fitted with 'fichures' or overlapping metal scales. These straps intersected over the horse's croup and were known as 'cruppers' and 'culieres'; they were light and decorative and gave good protection against slashing cuts of the sword.

Full bards continued to be produced for important clients up until the early 17th century. The French émigré, Etienne Delaune, took his skills as an armourer to Germany. Working in collaboration

JOUSTS (II)
1. 'Foreign' or 'Italian' jousting with lances (c.1520). The figure on the left of the picture is the Duke of Bavaria, and his opponent on the right is the Margrave of Brandenburg. As a rule three lances had to be broken in succession in this type of jousting. Henri II of France died because he insisted on breaking a fourth lance. He was killed not by the lance-head but by a splinter from the broken shaft of his opponent's lance. A 'manteau d'armes' fitted with a reinforcing bevor was worn for jousting with field lances. In Germany the *Freiturnier* (free tourney) was fought in the manner shown in our illustration, but between pairs of opponents instead of single combatants. 2. Sword combat. Note the ordinary field armour worn by the contestants (cf. fig. 1) and the 'rebated' swords without a point or a cutting edge. Each contestant carried a spare one in case his sword was lost or broken. The figure on the left of the picture is the Duke of Mecklenburg, and his opponent on the right is the Margrave of Brandenburg.

1

2

L.&F.
FUNCKEN

with the best craftsmen of his day he helped decorate many *de luxe* suits of armour, first in France and later in Germany, where his much-prized style was copied by armourers long after his death. The finest example of a decorated suit of armour in existence was made by Etienne Delaune (it can be seen illustrated on p. 71). It belongs to the collection in the Museum of Dresden.

The saddle

What is striking about the development of the saddle is the extent to which it ties in with changes in the lance – and not, as one might expect, with advances in the technique of horse-riding.

The appearance of the heavy lance coincided with the introduction of the 'chairback' cantle. The rider could lean back against this for support so as to gain the maximum possible thrust; the pommel at the front of the saddle curved over to form a kind of buckler that protected the abdomen and legs down to the knees. This piece of harness was sometimes called a 'German' saddle.

The saddle-back prevalent at the end of the 15th century gradually decreased in height and acquired distinctive 'wings'; these were fairly flexible and helped relieve the rider's fatigue. The 'bow' at the front of the saddle also began to decrease in size about this time.

As the lance grew lighter in weight, so the saddle-back gradually disappeared altogether. However, riders had taken to hanging their pistols from the protective bow on the saddle, and consequently it was only to go out of use when the first pistol holsters were introduced (these covered the rider's thighs and gave them some degree of protection). A typical feature of the second half of the 16th century were the small pads that were used to wedge the rider's thighs in position; these were placed behind the 'quarters' of the saddle.

The spur

In the past, several authors have attempted to classify the spur chronologically by studying one or other of its parts. Initially the rowel seemed to offer the most promising starting-point for such a study, but it has successfully foiled all attempts at classification, largely because of the number of its spikes

(this can vary from six to twenty, depending on the country and the period). The spur is, in fact, the trickiest item of the knight's equipment to date accurately.

The stirrup

Readers will find a large number of illustrations of stirrups in this volume. Let us simply point out here the existence of stirrup sabatons: these were worn from the mid to the late 15th century and covered most of the foot.

Great attention to detail was shown in the making of spurs – as, for that matter, in the making of all equipment, even down to the smallest buckle.

JOUSTS (III)
1. Helm in two parts (1490). 2. Helm in two parts (1515). 3. Extra-heavy armour (1490). A surprising feature is the unexpectedly graceful jointed waist. 4. Jousting sallet for use with field lances (1560). 5. Helm in three parts (early 16th century). 6. Double pieces for a heavy Saxon jousting armour (late 16th century). 7 and 8. Front and back view of a typical suit of armour from the period 1515–1520. It weighs nearly 41 kilos. The antennae-like projections on the shoulders were used for holding decorative lambrequins in position. 9. Jousting armour for use with field lances (1490). The legs of the wearer are protected by thigh-guards. The spike on the chest held a target (an apple, for example) which opponents would try and hit. To the right of fig. 9, a lance-head 3.20 metres long. 10. Helmet for use in light jousting – the so-called 'foreign' or 'Italian' joust (c.1500). 11. Armet for use in light jousting; it has a small opening for ventilation (1560). Some people still think this opening was designed (believe it or not) to allow the wearer to blow a trumpet without removing his helmet! 12. Armour (1500). 13. Armet for use in light jousting with an opening for ventilation. When the string was pulled the shutter opened (cf. fig. 11). 14. Helm (early 16th century).

1

2

3

4

5

ix F. Foncken

7

8

9

11

12

13

14

Jousts and tournaments

During the 16th century jousts and tournaments underwent a remarkable degree of development. Stricter rules were drawn up, and at the same time countless variations on them were introduced, particularly for jousting or combat with the lance.

Whereas in France the original warlike character of jousting was preserved, in Germany and the Low Countries a whole range of different exercises were devised. We shall try here to single out the most basic types.

The *Welsches Gesteck* or *Welsches Rennen* was an extremely popular form of jousting. It was also known as the 'foreign' or 'Italian' joust and it consisted of charging an opponent on the opposite side of the dividing barrier and trying to splinter his lance (this was made of poplar, and fairly light). The usual procedure was to fight a maximum of three opponents in succession. Although this may appear a relatively harmless feat to accomplish, it was in fact quite difficult as the head of the lance tended to skid off the smooth surface of the armour. It took a great deal of experience before a knight could successfully level his lance at the same time as controlling his mount (which was travelling at a gallop), then take aim and hit the right spot in his opponent's armour.

It was during an Italian joust on 30 June, 1559, that Henri II was mortally wounded. The king had already successfully splintered the traditional three lances, but he insisted on challenging an extra opponent, Gabriel de Montgoméry, lord of Lorges. Unfortunately, a splinter from Mongoméry's lance flew in through the sight of Henri's helmet and penetrated deep into the flesh below his right eyebrow. He died as a result of his injury on 10 July.

Accidents like this had become very rare in Italian jousting. By contrast, other versions of the joust that were being practised in Germany involved considerable risk for the participants. Jousts featuring the 'vanishing shield', the 'grill', the 'bourrelet', and the 'queue' (these were all discussed in Part I) were far more brutal and tended to be fought with pointed lance-heads instead of rebated ones.

Apparently these refined 'entertainments' became less frequent during the first half of the 16th century, and were eventually replaced by a single form of heavy jousting known as *Scharfrennen* (from *scharf*, meaning sharp, and *Rennen*, a race). As its name indicates, pointed lances mounted on strong shafts were used in this joust, which was quite different from the 'light' Italian jousting and far more spectacular. The aim of the joust was quite simply to unhorse one's opponent with these pointed lances, which were as deadly as anything used in battle. However we should mention here that we have come across lance-heads intended for use in this type of jousting that were far less dangerous.

The saddle used in the *Scharfrennen* had no cantle, so that the unhorsed opponent did not break his back. This did mean, of course, that there was nothing to impede a rider when he fell off his horse – but it is interesting to speculate on what happened to a body clad in armour, weighing in some cases as much as 50 kilograms, when it made sudden contact with the ground.

The term *stechen* (to sting) was also used in the late Gothic period to describe jousts in which the participants wore the 'frog-mouthed' helm and

JOUSTS (IV)

1. Double pieces for the joust (1540). 2. Armour (1580). This is a traditional field armour fitted with special reinforcing pieces for jousting: a manteau d'armes,[1] a pasguard, and a gauntlet called a 'gaignepain'. 3. Helm (1520). 4. Armet used for Italian jousting (1580). It has a lifting-peg on the visor (to hold it open) and a ventilation hole. 5. Field armour with reinforcing pieces for jousting (1520). 6. Armour for 'Italian' jousting (1520). 7. Armour (1560). 8. Field and jousting armour (1585). For a long time it was thought to belong to William the Conqueror! 9. Armour (1560). The true function of the ventilation hole is clearly shown here. The illustration shows how ridiculous the idea is of anyone blowing a trumpet while wearing a visor shaped like this (see figs. 11 and 13 on the previous plate). 10. Typical Saxon armour (1590).

[1] Translator's note: the piece illustrated here is in fact a grandguard.

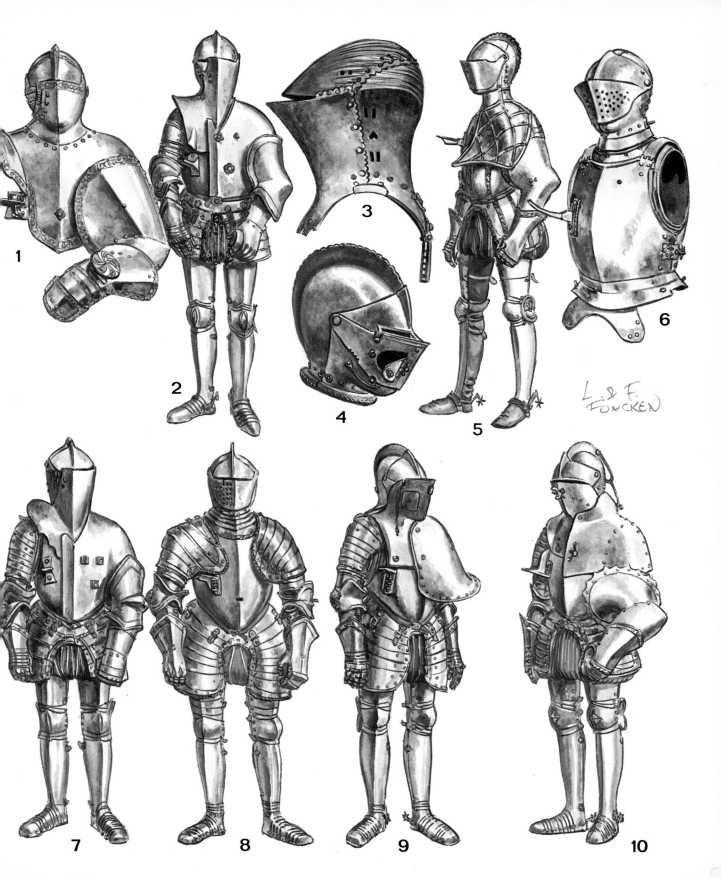

1

2

3

4

5

6

7

8

9

10

carried a heavy targe, frequently covered in leather. As a rule, lances with blunt heads were used in this type of jousting, but a number of marks have been found on armour and targes that could have been made by pointed lances.

Around 1515 a new kind of armour was introduced. This consisted of a helmet and body armour heavily reinforced with a 'manteau d'armes'; the legs were left completely unprotected. The barrier had, it is true, been considerably enlarged; it was now constructed of solid wood and in some cases was over 1.65 metres high. This noticeable trend towards ensuring greater and greater safety for the combatants is confirmed by the weight of suits of armour of the period, some of which were as heavy as 70 or even 80 kilograms. This was because contestants had to withstand blows from massive lances weighing between 10 and 15 kilograms.

The 'heavy' German joust evolved into the classic joust with full armour, manteau d'armes, and reinforced helmet. However, it is clear that the object of this type of jousting was simply to splinter the opponent's lance. When taking part in a 'light' joust, contestants wore traditional armour reinforced with supplementary pieces. These double pieces were removed for tourneys fought with the sword or for group combat.

The German *Freiturnier* or 'free tourney' was fought without a barrier between pairs of contestants. The procedure was first of all to splinter a lance, then for all participants to continue fighting with their swords.

As a result of the lance losing much of its prestige as a weapon during the first half of the century, tournaments rapidly went into a decline. They were finally abandoned for good in France in 1591, after Charles IX had been wounded in a fight with the Duke of Guise. At that period fluted hollow lances known as 'bourdonnasses' were being used.

Foot combat

Courtly foot combat was practised from the end of the 15th century onwards. The contest was fought on either side of a barrier so as to prevent participants from aiming low blows at one another. An ordinary suit of armour was worn in conjunction with a specially reinforced helmet that closed extra tight for greater protection.

At the beginning of the 16th century tonlet armour made its first appearance. This had a bell-shaped skirt that provided added protection for the legs.

The custom later grew up of adding reinforcing pieces to an ordinary suit of field armour. These could be bought as optional extras, and consisted of pieces like reinforced visors (instead of the special helmet that was usually worn) and a grandguard for the left shoulder and arm.

Only a very small number of special foot-combat armours have survived intact to this day. The finest examples were made between 1515 and 1520, the period when close-fitting costume armour was the main type being produced. The bend of the arms and legs was made completely impervious to blows by a system of jointed lamellai. The lower part of the actual trunk was completely enclosed in a pair of armoured 'breeches', so that the armour resembled a kind of diving-suit. A good-quality, perfectly smooth armour of this type was made in the newly-established workshop at Greenwich for Henry VIII, its royal patron. The fashion for costume armour was already over by around 1520.

JOUSTS (V)
1. Armet (1590). 2. Tonlet armour (1512). The laminated protection for the inner bend of the arm was called 'modern'. 3. Armour belonging to Henry VIII (1514). Its size indicates that the king's waist measurement at that time was approximately 88 cm. A later suit of armour made for him in 1540 measures 1.64 metres around the waist! 4. Tonlet armour of Henry VIII (1515). 5. Detailed view of helmet pictured in fig. 3. 6. Armet (1591). The lifting-peg used for holding open the visor during breaks in fighting often hung by a short cord, as shown here. 7. Armet-sallet (1490). At the period when the sallet reigned supreme this hybrid form also appeared. It combines the total protection of the armet with the typical slit visor of the universal sallet. 8. Costume armour (1515). 9. Savoyard burgonet (1610). The Germans nicknamed it *Todenkopf* (death's head). The only truly distinctive feature of foot-combat armours is the design of the visor, which restricts sight holes and ventilation holes to the smallest possible size.

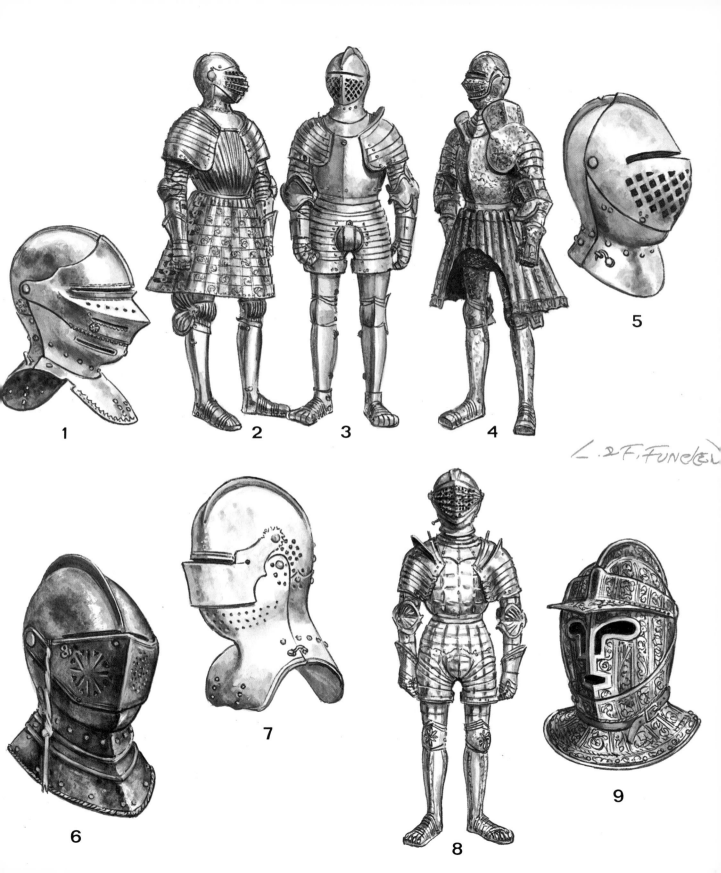

1

2

3

4

5

6

7

8

9

The last foot-combat armours that were made in the second half of the 16th century reverted to the style of the detachable tonlet skirt.

It is a curious fact that the suits that have survived to this day bear virtually no traces of the lethal blows their wearers were supposed to have received. In fact encounters of this kind would have been extremely exhausting for the participants, if only because of the impact of the blunt weapons on their armour. Would it be out of the question to imagine contestants fighting a duel of pure skill with wooden weapons?[1] At any rate this idea would offer one solution to the mystery of these undamaged harnesses.

Gauntlets and sabatons[2]

The illustrations of gauntlets and sabatons shown on the facing page are perfectly self-explanatory. We will therefore confine ourselves here to drawing the reader's attention to the 'knuckleduster' shape of many of the gauntlets and to the amazing locking system which could be used on occasion to take the weight of a weapon. The locking mechanism was operated by means of the thumb or fingers; in the latter case the edge of the mitten was fixed inside the wrist, over the guard.

Legend has attributed the introduction of the poulaine type of sabaton in the early 11th century to Falco IV, Count of Anjou, who had deformed feet, or alternatively to Henry II of England in the 12th century. In fact the poulaine was modelled on the contemporary civilian shoe known in the 16th century as a 'pigace' or 'pigache'; it had been worn and known about since classical times.

Similarly the 'bear's paw' or 'cow's muzzle' sabaton does not come from a supposed imitation of Charles VII's shoes (Charles had six toes on each foot); in any case, the style known as the 'demi-sabot' or 'demi-bear's paw' was worn from 1485 to 1490. The 'bear's paw' was to be replaced by the 'duck's beak' sabaton around 1550.

[1] Swords made of parchment and whalebone were sometimes used in tournaments.

[2] Translator's note: I have translated the French term *soleret* by 'sabaton'. An English equivalent of *soleret* does exist ('solleret') but it was rarely used before the 19th century and then (apparently) incorrectly.

GAUNTLETS AND SABATONS[3]

Gauntlets: 1. Mail mitten-gauntlet. 2. Gauntlet with metal roundels (1300). 3. Gauntlet with leather mitten (1300). 4 and 4a. Gauntlet made of lames (1320). This is the first crude precursor of the arming gauntlet. 5. Gauntlet with a metal-carpal plate separate from the fingers which are sewn onto the lining-glove (1325). 6. Gauntlet with separate metacarpal plate (1350). 7. *Idem* (1380). 8. 'Gothic' gauntlet (1440). 9. Mitten-gauntlet (1440). 10 and 11. 'Gothic' mitten-gauntlets with three and one lames respectively. 12. Mitten-gauntlet consisting of three lames (1460). 12a. Inside view of fig. 12. 13. Mitten-gauntlet (1470). 14. Mitten-gauntlet (1490). 15. Mitten gauntlet (1510). 16. 'Maximilian' mitten-gauntlet, joined to the lower cannon (1510). 17. Locking-gauntlet (1540). 18. 1560. 19. 1570. 20. 1595. 21. Artificial limb said to belong to Götz von Berlichingen. This legendary figure was mutilated in 1504 by a culverin ball, but a well-authenticated source gives an account of the amputation of his right hand. A detail (a) demonstrates how the articulation of the fingers worked. This 'iron hand' is not unique by any means. 22. 'Gothic' gauntlet (1480): a) cuff; b) wrist defence; c) metacarpal defence; d) finger defences in the shape of a knuckleduster. The gauntlet was attached to a lining-glove made of buckskin, doeskin, or elkhide; it was often reinforced under the palm and fingers.

Sabatons: 1. 1330. 2. 1350. 3. 1370. 4. 1384. 5. 1390. 6. Sabaton with detachable pointed toe-cap (poulaine). 7. Sabaton with poulaine (1450). 8. Sabaton with detachable poulaine (1450). 9. Sabaton with poulaine (1480). 10. 'Bear-paw' sabaton (1505). 11. Bear-paw sabaton (1510). 12. *Idem* (1515). 13. *Idem* (1530). This type of sabaton was sometimes called a 'cow's muzzle' sabaton. 14. 'Duck's beak' sabaton (1570). 15. *Idem* (1590).

When poulaines were popular in civilian fashion the length of these extensions was strictly regulated. Thus princes and dukes were entitled to wear poulaines measuring two and a half times the length of the foot; for the upper echelons of the aristocracy poulaines could be up to twice the length of the foot, and for knights they could be the same length as the foot. It is more than likely that this 'hierarchy of the poulaine' applied equally rigidly to military footwear.

[3] See Note 2.

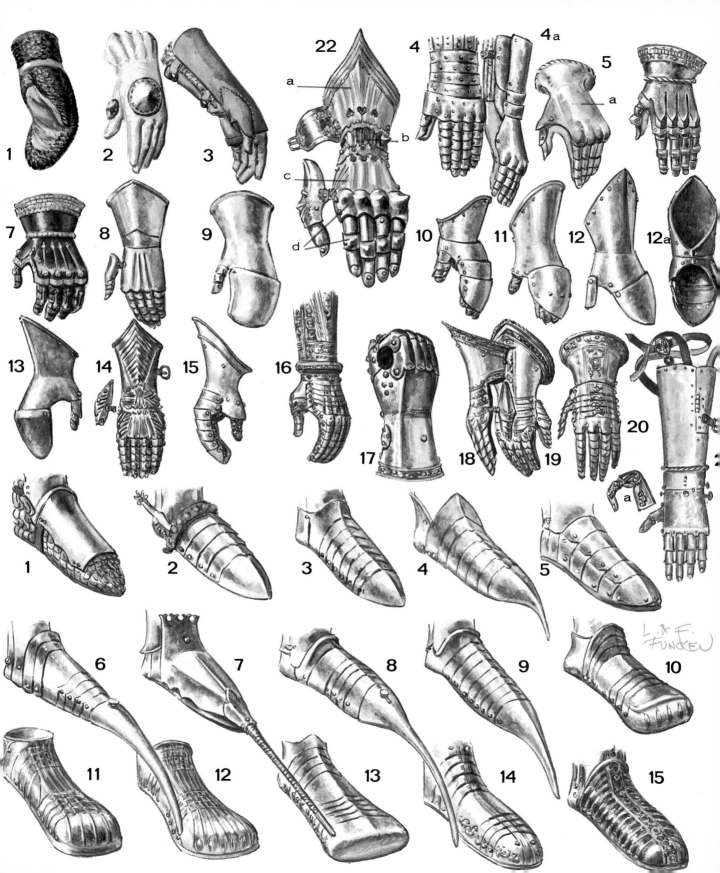

II HELMETS AND ARMOUR

Helmets

In Part I we broke off our survey of the development of the armet at the end of the 15th century. The models that followed in the 16th century can be divided into two distinct, though frequently confused types which we have christened the 'first type' and the close-helmet.

The 'first type' of armet

This 'first type' of armet carried on the features of the original model. These were:
1. the visor, which pivoted on two side fastenings;
2. the movable cheek-pieces. These were attached by side hinges and were bolted in position over the chin.

This system had one obvious weak point: the fastening where the cheek-pieces were joined was very fragile at the front and could be forced apart by a violent blow. It should be noted, however, that when the visor was lowered in position during action it functioned as a kind of extra fastening. It extended quite a way below the join of the cheek-pieces, and hence made it difficult to force apart the area of the helmet covering the jaw. It is not hard to imagine the torture a man-at-arms must have suffered when he was shut up for hours inside his armour; it only took the merest ray of sunshine beating on his suit for it to become unbearably hot. The 'first type' of armet had one advantage in that the wearer could leave it half-open until the very last minute during action, and so could get adequate ventilation. This is possibly the single useful feature that led to the open model of armet remaining in constant use until armour was finally abandoned.

The close-helmet

French is the only language that uses the same word to cover both the first and second types of armet; in English, Italian, and German the 'closed' model is rendered by the terms 'close helmet', *elmetto da incastro*, and *geschlossener Helm* respectively. It is interesting to note that although a clear distinction exists between the two types of helmet, there tends to be an extraordinary amount of confusion over which name to apply to the 'closed' armet, despite the fact that it is clearly differentiated and easily recognizable.

Several English and German experts confuse the open and closed models. According to them, as soon as the 'first type' of armet enters the 16th century it automatically becomes a close-helmet. The cause of this confusion seems to be the appearance of the comb and the crest,[1] which are supposedly charac-

THE ARMET
The 'first type' of armet shown here (the models date from 1450 to 1590) has the characteristic feature of side hinges and movable cheekpieces fastening over the chin (see Part 1, pp. 38 and 40). This type of helmet was to remain in use, together with the close-helmet, until the end of the 16th century. In the close-helmet all movable pieces were assembled at two side pivots (see following plate). It should also be remembered that a third system with a bevor and cheekpieces made in one piece and pivoting at the side on a hinge also existed (see Part 1, p. 40). The only likely explanation for the 'first type' of armet surviving such a long time is, we feel, the fact that it enabled the wearer to get some ventilation in hot weather by opening up the cheekpieces. With the close-helmet, or 'second type' of armet, however, the wearer had to completely bare his head.

1. 'Sparrow's beak' armet (1500): a) crown; b) sight; c) ventail (the sight and the ventail together, made up the visor, or *mezail*); d) bevor; e) lifting-peg; f) gorget or collar; g) rondel; h) cheekpieces; i) hole for crest-holder; j) the catch on the bevor.

2. Armet with bellows visor (1515). The bellows form was to last until around 1560. 3. 1520. 4. Sparrow's beak visor (1520). 5. Bellows visor (1530). 6. Visor shaped like a dog's snout (1520). 7. 'Monkey-face' visor (1525). 8. Bellows visor (1530). 9. With the lifting-peg in raised position (1535). 10. 1535. 11. With the visor pierced to form a grill (1555). 11a. The same helmet with the visor raised. 12. 1575. 13. 1590. The last two models have the characteristic profile of visors made by Greenwich armourers.

---

[1] Translator's note: Unlike some English experts, the authors use two different terms to describe the comb on the armet. The French word *crête* (crest) is used in the text to denote the low ridge-like comb, while *cimier* (comb) is reserved for the taller, more elaborate version.

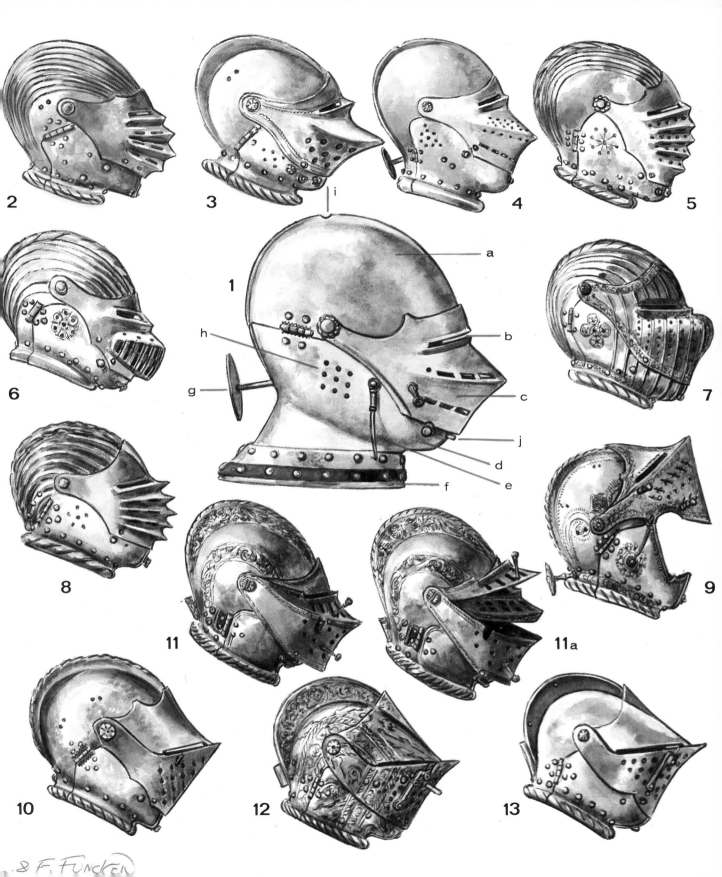

2

3

i

a

1

h

b

g

c

j

d

e

f

6

7

8

5

4

10

11

11a

9

12

13

8 F. FUNCKEN

teristic of the close-helmet. Now the 'first type' of armet undergoes a parallel development to the new arrival, the close-helmet. It follows the fashion, in a perfectly logical sequence, first for the low crest and later for the narrow, more slender comb. A glance at the illustrations will confirm this.

The only real difference between the 'first type' of armet and the close-helmet is the way both the visor and the bevor of the latter hinge *as a single unit* on the *same* side pivots.

Consequently the armet could no longer be opened over the chin. Instead it had to be opened from front to back by means of side-hinges to let the head through, and then closed up again, like the valves of a shellfish. It was then fastened at both sides of the neck with a pivot-hook or spring-catch. The only way of getting ventilation was to raise the visor; helmets were frequently fitted with visor supports, or lifting-pegs, to prevent the visor from falling forward as a result of the jolting caused by the horse's movements when on horseback.

The sallet-armet

In Part I we showed some of the hybrids that developed out of the classic 15th-century sallet with its impressive neckpiece. It was only to be expected that those who liked the sallet should try and adapt it to the fashion of the day by adding a visor (see Part 1, p. 37, fig. 8 and Part 2, p. 43, fig. 5).

The German *Vizierhelm*, which was actually a sallet fitted with a visor, hinged quite naturally in the same way as the close-helmet (see p. 53, fig. 2). When it was fitted with a bevor and gorget and a smaller, matching neckpiece it was known as a *Mantelhelm*.

This hybrid model (still based on the simple system of side pivots) spread throughout Europe from 1530 onwards and continued to be worn alongside the close-helmet proper until armour fell into disuse in the 17th century.

In France the armet belonging to the second half of the 16th century can be recognized by the slender shape of its raised crest; most foreign versions have noticeably thicker combs. This characteristic is a result of simplified techniques of forging which involved making the crown of the helmet in two parts. These were then crimped and riveted together under heat along the ridge of the comb. The great German and Italian armourers never resorted to what we can only call the underhand method of forging in a shell. This technique of forging meant the comb of the helmet could not be extended to form a narrow ridge that acted as a nasal between the two slits of the sight. This ridge fitted beneath the ventail, or upper bevor, and is found on all the finest foreign armets. In fact this slender bridge could not be made in the separate sections, and even armourers working with a single piece of metal tended to avoid the 'split sight' because of its relative fragility. The visor was made in two pieces, one with slits for the eyes and the other (the ventail) with

THE CLOSE-HELMET

The 'second type' of armet, otherwise known as the close-helmet, does away with the system of side hinges used in the true armet. Instead its visor (the sight plus the ventail) and bevor hinge on two side pivots. The helmet opened up like the two halves of a shell. It was fastened by means of a side pivot-hook or spring-loaded button. The Germans and Italians knew it as the *gaschlossene Helm* and *elmetto da incastro* respectively. However, these terms are only correctly applied very rarely, even in specialist works. Another method of classification based on the crest or comb that is supposedly typical of the close-helmet breaks down because of the presence of these features on armets of the 'first type' (see previous plate).

1. Armet with bellows visor (1510). 2. Hybrid form of sallet-armet (1510). This is a development of the sallet known as a *Vizierhelm* in Germany. 3. Armet with half-visor and sparrow's beak visor (1515). 4. Development of the hybrid model shown in fig. 3 (1515). This is the German *Mantelhelm* with its front and back gorget-plates. These can also be seen in figs. 5, 6, 8, 10, 12, 13, 14, 16 and 17. 5. Armet with an eagle's head visor (1530). 6. Monkey-face visor (1520). 7. Visor in the shape of a human face (1535). Although this armet is grouped together with the close-helmets that have visors in the shape of grotesque masks, the catch over the chin confirms it as belonging to the 'first type'. 8. Armet with visor shaped like a dog's head (1540). 9. Visor shaped like a human face (1520). The comb (seen in profile) is the same as the one in fig. 10. 10. With bellows visor (1540). 11 and 12. 1560. 13. 1570. The concave visor is typically English in style (it comes from the royal workshops at Greenwich). 14. With a visor made of a hinged animal's head (1580). Italy excelled in the *grande maniera* style which lasted from 1530 to 1590 and imitated classical Roman styles. 15. 1580. 16. Close-helmet with lifting-peg (1585). 17. 1585. 18. 1590. 19. 1592.

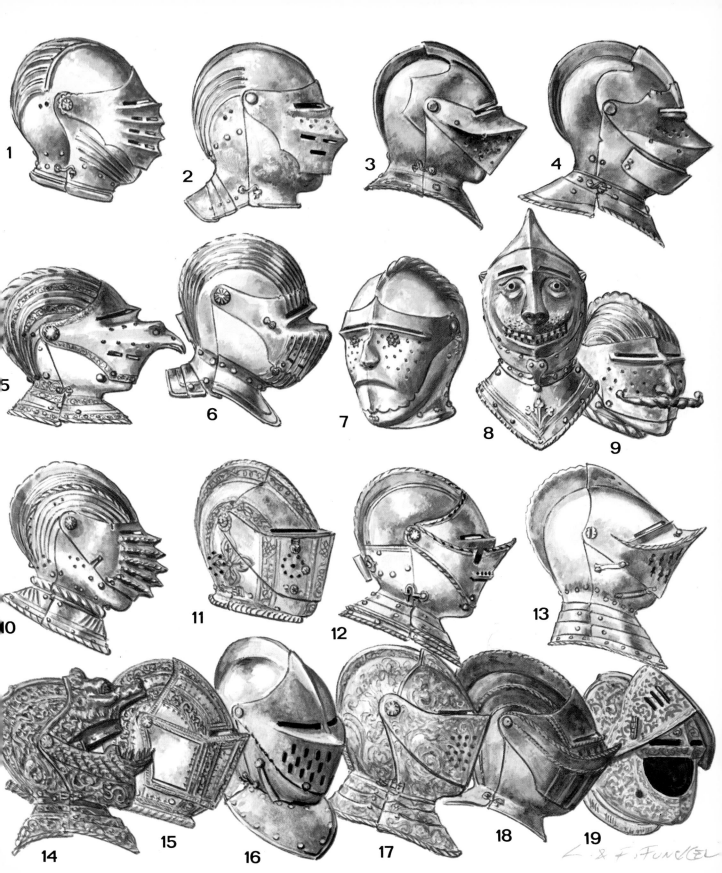

holes pierced for ventilation. This composite visor was fitted to the vast majority of armets and afforded excellent protection.

The rimmed armet

The rim method of securing the helmet was common to both the armet and the close-helmet. It consisted of a flange at the base of the helmet that fitted over a rim at the top of the gorget, or collar. This meant that the weight of the helmet was supported by the shoulders rather than the head. This rimmed armet was widely used on early 16th-century Maximilian armours, and remained in use until the following century.

Development of the armet

The hallmark of the age of the armet is the crest, and its successor, the comb; the latter was to become more and more elaborate as time went on. After 1590 the comb decreased in size and the shape of the visor grew bulkier. This change in outline was due to the visor becoming less prominent; at the same time the proportions of its lower part, the ventail, grew larger and the front edge became almost vertical. The details of these changes may seem rather complicated at first reading, but the illustrations give a very clear picture of what was happening.

Both public and private collections feature numerous examples of armets that have become separated from their original suit of armour. Apart from those models whose lavish decoration is a clear indication of their quality, it is always possible to tell a 'fine piece' by one small detail – the rope finish which, from the 15th century, was widely used to decorate the edges of the helmet. The workmanship of this cabling could range from a hasty going-over with a file to the most delicate chiselwork.

The face armet

During the period between 1510 and 1540, when Maximilian armour was being made, a few rare examples of armets appeared that had visors in the form of a grotesque representation of the human face. The most famous example of these was made around 1512 by the celebrated armourer Conrad Seusenhofer of Innsbruck. To this day it still astonishes and amuses visitors to the Tower of London. The helmet represents a face sneering in a very lifelike manner; the features are emphasized by cleverly-placed ventilation slits.

This curious piece was said to belong to Henry VIII's jester, though there is no strong evidence for this. It is decorated with a pair of ram's horns and apparently was originally fitted with a pair of spectacles that no longer survive today.

Most of these astonishing creations were made in Nuremberg. It had a far greater output than Innsbruck, Augsburg, or Milan, mainly because of the work of mastercraftsmen like Wilhelm von Worms the Elder.

During the same period animal heads were widely featured by all workshops. The customers who were interested in these more fanciful designs seem to have been almost exclusively German.

After 1530 the Italian *gran maniera* period, with its characteristic 'Roman' armours, took over. This era has left us with an impressive range of pieces of every

THE BURGONET (I)

1. First half of 16th century. 2. Burgonet with movable visor and triple crest (first half of 16th century). The holes for attaching its cloth covering are just visible. The same applies to fig. 5 (see also next plate, figs. 4 and 7). 3. Mid-16th century. This burgonet was sometimes called a *pot-en-tête* (literally, 'pot-on-the-head'). 4. Triple-crested burgonet (second half of 16th century). Note the curious resemblance to the characteristic shape of the morion. It has been given the name of 'burgonet-pot'. 5. This 'pot-on-the-head' demonstrates the latter stages of the development of the burgonet proper (second half of 16th century). 6. Second half of 16th century. 7. Landsknecht standard-bearer and double-pay pikemen (*c.*1525). These were élite troops fighting in the front line. Very few examples survive of the type of burgonet they are wearing. Their pikes were about 3.75 metres long.

In France, an ordinance of 1534 granted infantry the right to wear the 'crested sallet', which soon became known as the 'Burgundian headpiece' and was eventually christened the 'burgonet'. The immense popularity of this new military headgear is easily explained by its unusually graceful lines, which were attractive and functional at the same time.

1

2

3

4

5

7

6

L. & F.Funcken

type, all of them displaying extraordinary inventiveness and richness of execution. These armours had virtually nothing in common with actual military equipment; they seem to have been intended more for actors taking part in the early tragedies which Italy, during this fertile period of the Renaissance, had just introduced to Europe.[1]

The burgonet

At the beginning of the 10th century the burgonet, which grew out of the Italian barbute and the sallet, was known as the 'Burgundian headpiece'. It was taken up both by the *Knappen* (men-at-arms of the feudal German lords) and by the famous land-sknechts, who knew it by the name of *Sturmhaube* (literally, assault helmet).

The burgonet has several distinctive features, notably its 'fall', or horizontal visor; its 'cheeks', 'lugs', or 'cheek-guards'; and its clearly-marked neckguard. This extremely functional helmet followed the example of the armet, which was worn by high-ranking fighting men, and gradually acquired a decorative low crest that later developed into a tall comb.

No previous military headpiece had been as practical and, at the same time, as attractive as the burgonet. It is fascinating to see its shape evolve until it acquires a degree of military elegance that has never been equalled. The great lords knew what they were about when they ordered burgonets from their master-armourers and had them decorated by the leading artists of the day.

These magnificent pieces are preserved in our museums today, most of them with their barred or bellows-shaped faceguard or buffe[2] still intact. These pieces were designed to protect the faces of the distinguished noblemen who wore them. However, despite all the skill of mastercraftsmen and artists that went into making them, these additional pieces somehow do not look right on the burgonet, and they simply serve to remind us of the distinctive armet visor they were modelled on.

The burgonet reached the height of its popularity in the mid-16th century, and after this date it began to be made out of thin, light metal. It was mass-produced in the workshops of Nuremberg and Augsburg, and eventually developed from an infantry headpiece to become a light cavalry helmet that was worn by troops all over western Europe.

Some very fine-quality models of burgonet had three to five combs and were designed to take a cloth headdress as well. It has often been claimed that helmets of this type were intended to be worn by chamois hunters, as they were equipped with a non-reflecting cover and gave protection against falling stones. This seems to us to be an extremely risky hypothesis, since it is a known fact that a considerable number of troops wore burgonets of this type, in particular the personal bodyguard of the Emperor Charles V in 1530.

THE BURGONET (II)
1. Burgonet with pivoting visor (*c*.1560). 2. *Circa* 1600. 3. Late 16th century. 4. Triple-crested burgonet (early 16th century). The pairs of holes for attaching the cloth covering can be seen in the illustration (see fig. 7).

Hybrid forms of the burgonet: 5. Pot-burgonet (mid-16th century). 6. So-called 'Hungarian' type (mid-16th century). 7. Morion-burgonet with five crests (1560). A fabric covering was fairly commonly used on helmets of this type, either to cut down reflection or as a means of identification. 8. Morion-burgonet (1570). 9. Morion-burgonet (1600). 10. Cabasset-burgonet (1550).

11. Princely armour. There are countless full-length portraits in existence that show armour-clad figures with their head and legs unprotected. Today they are described as wearing half-armour or foot-combat or tilt armour. We tend to think that armour was depicted in this fashion mainly for aesthetic reasons, in order to play down the warlike aspect of the portrait. It is highly unlikely that fighting men would have been prepared to face the hazards of combat wearing such basic equipment. The burgonet shown in this figure was frequently an 'optional extra' that could be bought at the same time as the full armour with, of course, its stiflingly hot but indispensable close-helmet. The reader can find an example of the half-armour that was actually worn below; it includes the typical 'peascod' breastplate of the period.

---

[1] Tragedies, incidentally, that had as little to do with Classical antiquity as the armours.
[2] Translator's note: The term 'buffe' is used in English to describe the bevor at this period. (See note to p. 58)

1

2

3

4

5

6

7

8

9

10

11

The Savoyard burgonet

This burgonet utilized the same defensive principle as the burgonet with face-guard mentioned earlier. It was a hybrid version of the close-helmet and the burgonet, and had the latter's 'fall', hinged on side pivots, as well as the bevor with gorget-plates.[1]

The faceguard was suspended from the same pivots as the visor of the movable fall, and could be raised or lowered by means of this. This metal plate was very simply, not to say crudely, made, and had nothing in common with the classic visor – except, of course, its protective function. It had large sight-holes cut out of it and tiny holes pierced for ventilation.

Armourers went to considerable lengths to contrive new ways of giving this defensive piece more 'personality'. Sight-holes in the shape of eye sockets were opened up and a triangle was cut out to represent a mouth. The striking effect this achieved was emphasized in some cases by the addition of eyelids, eyebrows (made by following the curve of the edges of the fall), nostrils, noses, or mouths (made out of wide slits). In Germany this terrifying mask was sometimes called a *Todenkopf*, or death's head mask.

This type of helmet is generally classified as an armet (although in our opinion its fall makes it more of a burgonet). It was usually very crudely made out of rough, blackened sheet metal. The Italians distinguished it from the armet by calling it *elmetto alla viscontea*. The wholly Italian version introduced by the troops of Charles Emmanuel of Savoy enjoyed a fair measure of success in the specialized area of de luxe armours. It lasted throughout the period of *armatura da corazza* (cuirassier armour) which was worn by one or two great lords in the first half of the 17th century.

The morion

The name 'morion' is derived either from the Spanish *morro* (meaning the top of the skull or a rounded body) or, more simply perhaps, from *More* or *Maure* (meaning a Moor). The morion in any case has the alternative name of 'Moorish helmet'. Whatever the correct etymology, the morion was to oust all other types of helmet during the 16th century. It first appeared in France around 1510 and is mentioned in royal ordinances from the time of Henri II to Charles IX, i.e., from 1547 to 1574.

The original morion seems to have had a low, hemispherical crown with a low crest, perfectly in keeping with the style of other helmets of the period. We have tried unsuccessfully to base some sort of chronological classification of the morion on the changing shape of its crown as it gradually progressed through the various stages of low, medium, and high, but we have to admit that only the comb shows any noticeable tendency to increase in size. Even then this variation in height is in no way systematic; there are numerous examples of late 16th-century morions with a low crown and only a slightly-raised comb.

The number of good-quality morions on display in our museums today is an indication of the popularity of this helmet among European infantry. In Germany the morion even managed to supplant the popular *Sturmhaube* which was worn by the warlike landsknechts. There is evidence, however, of some resistance to the introduction of the morion.

THE BURGONET (III)
1. 'Roman'-style Italian burgonet (1541). 2 and 3. 1540. 4. *Circa* 1580. 5. Roman-style Italian burgonet (1560). 6. *Idem* (1589). 7. *Idem* (1586). 8. Italian burgonet in baroque style (early 17th century).

9. Standard-bearer of the Duke of Milan, wearing a half-armour for an infantry officer *alla tedesca* (in the German style), (c.1525). The burgonet has a pivoting visor, or fall, which appears to serve little purpose. In any case it was soon to be superseded by later developments in this type of helmet.

---

[1] This is the bevor covering the entire lower area of the helmet and enclosing the cheeks and chin; it is not to be confused with the bevor, or 'buffe', of the burgonet.

2

3

4

6

7

9

8

L. & F. FUNKEN

We have found an astonishing example of a hybrid burgonet made around 1560 which seems to be a clever compromise between the old and the new styles of headgear (see plate II on burgonets, p. 57, figs. 7, 8, 9).

Even officers of senior rank did not consider it beneath them to wear the morion, and colonels and *mestres de camp* regularly donned it when they went to face enemy infantry. The helmet was gilded, chiselled, and generously plumed in accordance with the rank of its wearer. It had to be 'proof', that is, impervious to an arquebus ball, and had to weigh an average of 2 kilos. The 'reinforced morion' was worn by élite halberdiers entrusted with guarding the ensign, and by lieutenants and captains of pikemen.

The superb specimens of the morion that have come down to us take our breath away with the delicacy and sheer variety of their decoration. The most amazing point about them, however, is the incredible skill of the armourers who managed to hammer these elegant helmets (comb included) out of a single piece of rough metal! We can imagine the contrast there must have been between these and the wretched pieces produced at the end of the century, which were made in two separate parts out of blackened sheet metal that resisted polishing.

The morion cabasset

The morion cabasset appeared at the same period as the classic morion and was differentiated from it by the fact that it had no comb. Instead, protection was afforded to the wearer by the sloping ogival lines of the high crown, which edged weapons were unable to get any purchase on.

The morion cabasset is far rarer than the morion and appears to have been worn mainly by mounted troops. A soldier on horseback would, after all, have been more exposed than an infantryman to the possibility of being involved in a swordfight where it would have been only too easy for a backhanded cut to catch on the tall comb of the morion. In any case, there is clear evidence that light cavalry always preferred to wear more compact helmets like the burgonet.

The morion cabasset, or German *Birnmorion* (literally, 'pear morion') was often called a 'Spanish morion'.

The cabasset

The cabasset, or German *Birnhelm* (literally, 'pear helmet') was shaped like the calabash and probably took its name from it too. Together with the morion, it achieved wide popularity, but because it was simpler to make, it managed to completely oust its far more elegant rival after the end of the 16th century.

The cabasset was worn by all types of footsoldier. It was the sole protection worn by the arquebusier, who was already heavily weighed down with his equipment and his weapon. The musketeer, on the other hand, had to carry a heavy musket, plus the all-important fork rest and a baldric for cartridges;

THE MORION

The morion was far more widespread than either its rival, the cabasset, or the hybrid version of it known as the morion-cabasset. The countless examples that have come down to us (ranging from the plainest to the most elaborate models) testify to the enormous popularity of this helmet.

Morion with low crown: 1. 1560. 2. *Circa* 1600. 3. 1580. 4. Late 16th century. Figures 1, 2 and 4 (as well as fig. 13) are made out of two separate pieces crimped and riveted together. Note that the fleur-de-lys motif was not necessarily an indication of French origin. In fact these are mass-produced German helmets.

Morions with a high crown: 5 and 6. 1570. 7. 1580. 8. Late 16th century. 9. Second half of 16th century. 10. 1580.

Morions with crown of medium height: 11. 1580. 12. 1600. 13. 1600. The town of Passau was famous for morions of this type. 14. Steeply-curved morion (*c.*1580). 15. Morion with tall crest (mid-16th century). The thing to note in this helmet is not its etched decoration, but the amazing virtuosity of the master-armourer who was able to forge it in one piece.

The generally received idea that the comb grew progressively taller in the course of the 16th century is well and truly contradicted by the examples shown here. The varying height of the crown of the helmet cannot be used as an indication of date either. One thing is certain, however, and that is the dramatic decline in quality that took place during the last years of the century; the only exceptions to this rule were *de luxe* helmets.

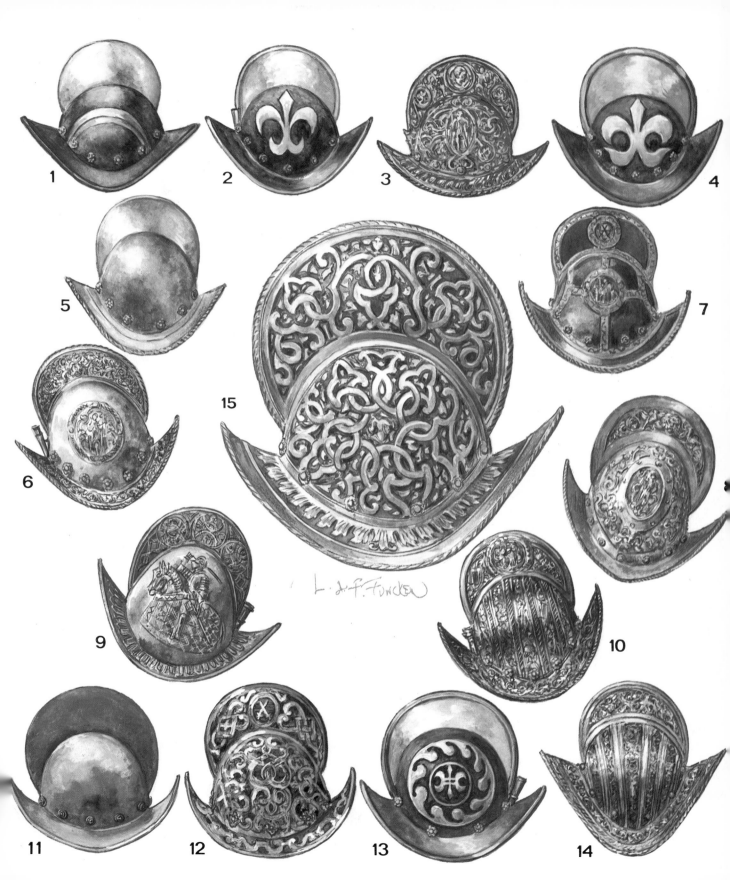

1

2

3

4

5

6

7

15

9

10

11

12

13

14

L. & F. Funcken

as a result, he very soon got rid of the cabasset and took to wearing a broad felt hat instead. Both of these specialist soldiers had little to fear from mounted troops, as they could withdraw behind the safety of the pikes whenever the cavalry looked threatening.

The plain outlines of the cabasset, which were occasionally relieved by a small comb, took on a rather unprepossessing appearance once it began to be manufactured by industrial methods at the end of the 16th century. First it lost its stalk-shaped spur, then its domed crown. Out of these changes was born a pitiful runt that was baptized with the name of the household utensil it resembled – the pot.

Armour

In Part 2 we showed the gradual development of armour up to the mid-15th century, the date when it reached its apogee. The following century was to mark the decline of the armourer's art, as it became sacrificed to the tyrannical demands of fashion and was irresistibly superseded, despite desperate efforts, by a new and terrible invention.

A race grew up between bullets and armour-plating – a race which was lost before it had begun. The 'villainous weapon', the firearm, inexorably gained the upper hand and gradually destroyed the superior position that physical strength, skill, and bravery had once held in war. Henceforth the old knighthood in their shining armour were a vulnerable target. They had to stand by and watch as one of the bases of their traditional power crumbled away in the face of an infantry they could no longer even break through – after they had blithely (and literally) ridden roughshod over it for so many centuries. The superb gendarmeries had to reconcile themselves – not without some bitterness – to learning obedience, the fundamental law of modern warfare. Feudal lords, ruined by long wars, ceased fighting on their own behalf and hired out their services instead, finally disappearing for good when the first cavalry regiments were set up.

Round armour

Following on the 'Gothic' style mentioned in Part 2, there appeared at the beginning of the 16th century a type of smooth armour that was virtually an exact copy of models belonging to the second half of the previous century. The only differences were its laminated tassets, its heavier gauntlets and, notably, its rounded sabatons.

This Italian armour enjoyed a limited popularity everywhere in Europe apart from Germany, where a very different style with a convex chest already existed.

Transitional armour

This was a style of armour with a distinctive globular breastplate; like the previous style, it first appeared in Germany at the beginning of the century. The cuff of the gauntlets was straight-edged, while the sabatons were in the 'bear-paw' style that copied a contemporary civilian shoe. This style was allegedly made fashionable by Charles

THE MORION-CABASSET

This type of helmet (also known as a 'Spanish morion') combined a pear-shaped skull with the curved brim of the morion. It was, in fact, a perfect cross between the morion and the cabasset. Judging by the relatively few specimens that have survived compared with the huge number of morions that fill our large museums, this elegant helmet was never particularly popular. The spur on top of the helmet always pointed backwards. If it had pointed in the opposite direction it would have got in the way of blows from edged weapons. The rivets and bosses held the hat worn inside the helmet in position; this was made of rawhide or buckskin. The plume-holder was optional.

1. Early 16th century. 2. 1580. 3. Morion-cabasset with cheekpieces in the form of a chinstrap (mid-16th century). 4 and 5. 1580. 6. *Circa* 1600. 7. 1580. Its decoration is a crude imitation of that shown on the helmet in the next figure. 8. 1580.

9. Halberdier wearing a morion-cabasset and the corselet, or infantryman's half-armour (1570). A good-quality Italian armour like this one could weigh between 12 and 18 kilos, depending on how resistant it was to bullets. Sometimes only the helmet was 'proof' (i.e. bullet-proof).

1

2

4

5

6

7

8

9

L. &F. Fonken

VII of France, who wore it to disguise a foot deformity.[1]

This smooth armour was thought to be too out of keeping with the heavily-worked style fashionable at that period, and it soon began to acquire a surface decoration of fluting. Decoration was at first limited to zigzag motifs over the chest, but was later extended to cover virtually every part of the armour.

Maximilian armour

Thus, shortly after 1500, there appeared the distinctive German armour that was named after the wealthy Emperor Maximilian. This name was, in fact, a rather arbitrary choice, since most 'Maximilian' armours were made long after the emperor's death in 1519. However, it is fair to say that Maximilian did give a powerful impetus to the industry of the German *Plattner* when it was challenged by fierce competition from Italian armourers.

In the past all good-quality armour had been attributed first to Italy, and then to Germany.[2] The truth, in fact, is more complicated than this. Milan, it is true, did dominate the production of armour from the 15th to the 17th centuries owing to a combination of industrialized forging techniques and business methods that would have done credit to our leading firms today. However, the workshops of Nuremberg put up stiff competition against Milan throughout the entire period between the early 15th and mid-16th centuries – the period when the great Bavarian centre began manufacturing 'munition' armour. Augsburg also rose to eminence with the work of the Helmschied family and the decoration of artists like Dürer and Burgkmair.

---

[1] See 'Gauntlets and sabatons', p. 48.
[2] In 1859 Auguste Demmin took the lead in restoring to German armourers the credit for work that had hitherto been regarded as Italian in origin – even in Germany, where his findings were greeted with scepticism by museum curators. Ten years later, the convictions of the hot-headed pioneer turned out to be amply confirmed, and thus the great German masters re-emerged from obscurity. Demmin, however, got rather carried away and declared the majority of weapons and armours kept in arsenals and museums to be of German make; he restricted Italian dominance to the fields of ceramics and mosaics only. The famous 'Hercules' armour in the museum of Dresden – possibly the finest in existence – was pronounced to be of German origin by Demmin, whereas in fact it was forged in Sweden and decorated by an Antwerp craftsman after drawings by the Frenchman Delaune (see p. 71).

As for fluted armour, this was copied by the Italians, who had no intention of letting even the smallest fraction of the market be taken from them without a fight. Production of fluted armour was abandoned by Milan in 1520, and afterwards it continued its career in its native country, Germany, until 1540. Nuremberg was the main centre of production; Innsbruck and Augsburg were never to equal it, at any rate in terms of output.

Costume armour

From the beginning of the century a parallel development in armour was taking place. By this period Maximilian armour, with its characteristic fluting, was already simulating the folds of clothing, albeit in a stylized fashion. However, a new armour was being made that reproduced with far greater accuracy the slashed doublets and knee-breeches that were in fashion at the time. Skilful engraving was used to imitate the effect of the fabric (either

THE CABASSET
1. Etched cabasset with spur (late 16th century). Few examples of the cheekpieces, which are made of laminated metal, have survived to the present day. Ordinary models were sometimes fitted with a simple leather chinstrap. The spur tapers off towards the back of the helmet and always points towards the plume-holder. 2. Chiselled cabasset with spur (1580). 3. Etched cabasset with spur (1580). 4. Chiselled cabasset with spur (late 16th century). 5. Embossed cabasset with a twin spur (1580). 6. Burnished cabasset with a serrated crest (1530). 7. Embossed cabasset made of leather, without a spur (late 16th century). 8. Embossed cabasset, with spur (late 16th century). 9. Burnished cabasset, without spur (first half of 16th century). 10. Cabasset, without spur (early 17th century). 11. Cabasset with half-crest (early 17th century). 12. Cabasset with full crest (early 17th century).

13. Arquebusier wearing a cabasset; from an engraving by Jacob de Gheyn included in the *Wapenhandelinghe* (*Handling of Weapons*), published in 1608. The part of the firing drill shown here consists of fixing the match over the serpentine.

1

2

3

4

5

6

7

8

9

10

11

12

13

damask or velvet) that showed through the 'slashes'[1] of civilian clothes.

As civilian fashion moved towards clothes with fuller sleeves, imitations of this kind were no longer possible. However the Waffensammlung in Vienna has in its collection an armour with enormous puffed sleeves dating from 1520 and bearing the signature of the armourer Kolmann Helmschied.

Parade armours were worn in conjunction with armets with a visor in the form of a grotesque representation of a human face. These faces were sometimes set off with a pair of spectacles or even, in some cases, an imitation of a drip at the nose!

Matching helmets were provided for jousting and field armours. This practice, in fact, was to be adopted for all subsequent types of armour.

The development of armour

In Part 2 we presented the development of armour in tabular form. This saved us from having to go into too much detail in the text, but in any case the numerous examples given in the illustrations mean we can dispense with long explanations. Below is the continuation of this chronological table of armour, covering the period of the 16th century.

Date	Armour	Helmet
c.1500	Transitional 'round' armour, followed by 'Maximilian' armour with narrow fluting and distinctive smooth greaves. Disappearance of the pointed sabaton. Introduction on large scale of mitten-gauntlet.	'First type' of armet
c.1510	Introduction of 'costume' armours.	
c.1512	First complete protection for the inside of the elbow-joint achieved by means of laminations.	

ARMOUR (I)
1. 'Round' armour marking the transition between the 'Gothic' and the 'Maximilian' styles (1500). The helmet is an armet of the 'first type' (see the plate on the armet). 2. Pre-Maximilian armour with bellows visor (1505). 3. Costume armour with a visor in the shape of a face-mask (1510). 4. Italian armour *alla tedesca*; the sallet-armet has a bellows visor (1510). 5. 'Classic' Italian armour (1510). This suit is in the great tradition of the 15th century, which was still very popular at the time. 6. Maximilian armour with 'monkey-face' visor (1515). 7. Maximilian armour with bellows visor (1520). This is a 'featherweight' suit weighing only 18.79 kilos. 8. Maximilian armour (1520). 9. Armour with 'monkey face' visor and domed breastplate (1530). This 'Gansbauch' or 'brisket' form of breastplate is characteristic of the period. 10. Costume halfarmour (1530). Note the cuirass rest placed on the wearer's left, for a left-handed man.

[1] Both Maximilian and costume armour left the greaves, or shin defences, smooth in imitation of the stockings called *bas-de-chausses* worn by civilians at the period.

Cuirasses had been painted since the 12th century, but the discovery of painting in oils in the 14th century gave a new impetus to this style of applied decoration.

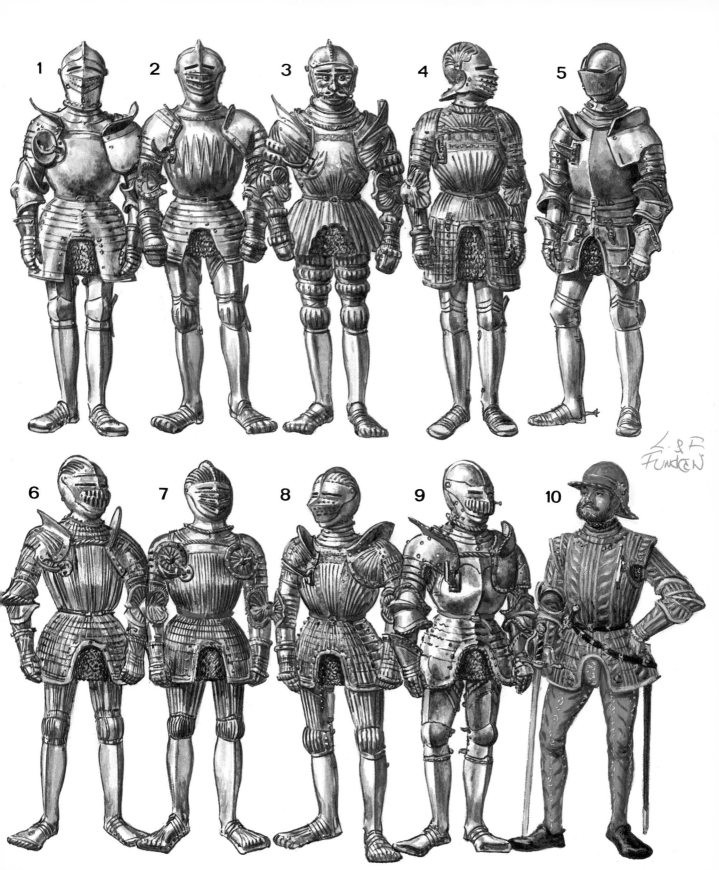

Date	Helmet	Armour
c.1515	Introduction of 'three-quarter' armour with no greaves. Founding of the armoury at Greenwich.	
c.1520	Production of fluted armour ends in Italy.	Close helmet joins 'first type' of armet.
c.1530	Introduction of globular breastplate with medial ridge in the shape of a 'brisket' or 'goose belly' (*Gansbauch*). Re-introduction of fingered gauntlet for use with pistol; however, mitten-gauntlet continues in regular use. Introduction of blackened or blued armours and Italian 'Roman' armours.	Introduction of burgonet with sides similar to those on armet and close-helmet.
c.1540	Disappearance of fluted armour in Germany.	
c.1550	Globular breastplate lengthens to take on 'peascod' or 'long-bellied' form. Introduction of cuirasses with tassets forming 'cuisses'.	
c.1570	The rounded breastplate lengthens to a 'goose-belly' shape and becomes humped in imitation of the civilian 'Polish doublet'. First Elizabethan armours made at Greenwich.	
c.1580	Introduction of rounded tassets over the hips and laminated tassets extending to the knees; cuisses almost completely discarded.	
c.1590	Disappearance of Italian 'Roman' armours.	

ARMOUR (II)

1. Maximilian armour with face-mask visor (1530). This type of armour was made at Innsbruck, Augsburg, and even Milan, though by far the greatest number of suits were forged at Nuremberg. Production of Maximilian armour was completely abandoned around 1540, although at least one more suit of this style was made about 1557 for the future emperor, Maximilian II. 2. Costume armour of Spanish style (1538). 3. 1540. 4 and 5. 1550. 6. 1560. 7. 1570. The fact that the cuirass rest was omitted from suits of armour with growing frequency (see also fig. 10) is an indication of the decreasing role of the lance. 8. Armour and armet with a half-visor (1585). 9. 1595. 10. 1595. Note the decorative fabric trimming known as 'pickadils' (hence the origin of the name 'Picadilly'). These had been in use for at least fifty years. The old half-visor is evidently still popular.

Figs. 3 and 9 have a burgonet and buffe.

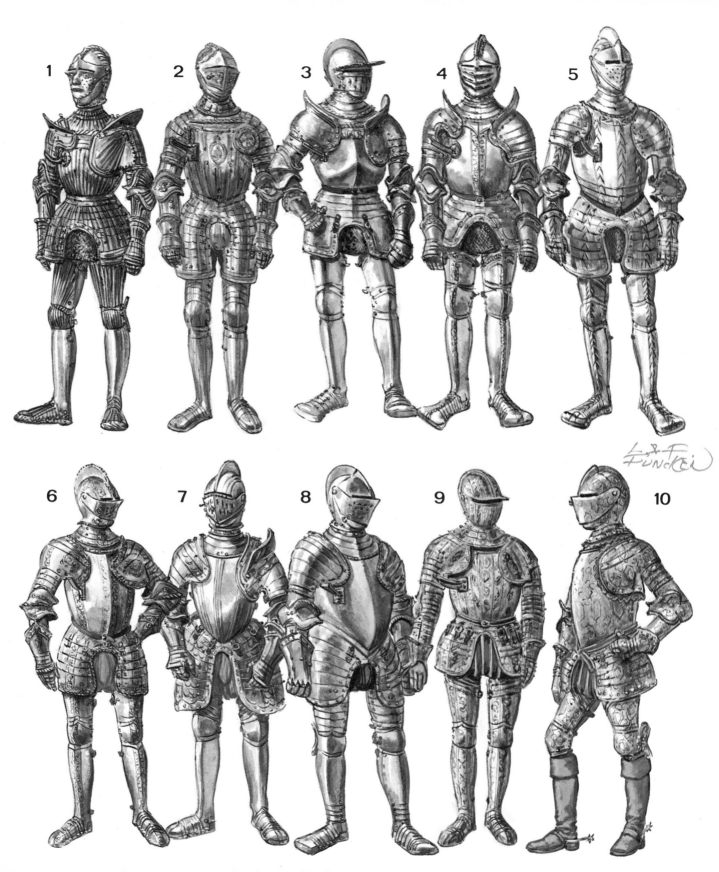

It should be noted that alongside the really fashionable armours with their clearly differentiated features there existed a vast assortment of outdated styles that were often up to twenty or thirty years old. Despite their age and their unfashionableness, however, people carried on wearing them in the (quite understandable) interest of avoiding unnecessary expense.

Classical armour

After the highly individual armours of the early 16th century, taste shifted back towards more conventional styles decorated with bands of engraving of ever-increasing width.

In the case of ordinary armour this decoration was relatively crude, being simply etched with acid. However, on quality armour it occasionally attained the heights of artistic perfection. The Germans, despite their skill as engravers, never equalled the standards of the Italian masters in embossed work, though towards the end of the century they did produce some quite outstanding suits of de luxe armour. These were copied by French craftsmen working on de luxe armour for Henri II – who was, incidentally, probably the greatest collector of armour ever.

The decoration of armour

From the first introduction of full armour the smooth surface of the plackart had been decorated with motifs and coats of arms picked out in different colours of varnish. Later on, after the end of the 14th century, actual paint was used. The poor durability of this type of decoration rapidly led to its being supplanted by engraved designs incised with a burin. The motifs used consisted of Christian symbols and series of initials (generally as baffling as the ones found on sword-blades) engraved across the upper part of the chest; they had, of course, the advantage that they could not be erased.

The heavily-ribbed Gothic armours from Germany were decorated with fairly crude engraved work. Italy, as a contrast to the sinewy, spiky style of its great rival, evolved a style of round, sculpted armour that had no ornamentation.

In the 16th century the powerful current of the Renaissance directed all the techniques of artistic production to the decoration of armour. Costume armour was ornamented with bands of openwork that allowed the gorgeous fabric underneath to show through. This style of decoration was one of the first examples of chiselling done on silver-gilt.

Decorative techniques: etching, chiselling, niello, damascening, and embossing

These five decorative techniques frequently get confused – particularly chiselling and engraving.

Etching
This, the oldest and simplest method of decoration, was borrowed from the etchers of prints of the previous century. The craftsman would draw his subject with a scraper directly onto the surface of the piece that was to be decorated, which had previously been coated with laquer. The metal area left exposed was then eaten away by acid, leaving a recessed design. In order to make the design stand out more clearly the channels left by the acid were

ARMOUR (III)
Parade armour of Eric XIV of Sweden (c.1565). The horse is protected by a complete set of bards of 'skirt' or 'tonlet' armour: chanfron (defence for the head), crinet, picière or peytral (defence for the chest), crupper, and flanchards (defences for the flanks.

The particularly lavish decoration on this suit of armour represents six battle scenes from the Trojan War and the story of the Argonauts. The horse bards are decorated with fourteen scenes depicting the labours of Hercules. The craftsman responsible for the decoration was Eliseus Libaerts of Antwerp. His work was based on the drawings of Etienne Delaune of Orléans, whose 'little ornaments' were much sought-after and extensively copied on many other *de luxe* armours.

Ironically, Eric XIV never took delivery of his superb suit of armour – in our opinion the finest of its kind ever made. It was intercepted on its way to Eric by his enemy, the King of Denmark, and was sold off to Christian II, the Elector of Saxony, in 1603.

filled with varnish. When this was heated it showed up black against the polished background of the armour.

Obviously the final result depended entirely on the skill of the etcher. The design itself could range from a very ordinary depiction of scenery to the most elaborate tableaux representing human figures. Particularly attractive effects could be obtained by picking out the outlines of design in gold and silver on a background of blued steel. This technique, which was widely used in Germany, was known as *Goldschmelz* (from *Gold*, meaning gold, and *Schmelz*, meaning enamel).

Etching could also be done by painting a reversed image of the required design in laquer. The design was completely covered in a protective coating so that its outlines were thrown into relief and it stood out from its background, which was completely eaten away by the acid. The results obtained by this technique looked convincing enough from a distance, but when they were viewed from close up telltale flaws could be seen along the edges of the designs. Of course these defects could always be touched up afterwards with a burin, but this required long hours of work by an experienced engraver – and meant that costs rose prohibitively. On the other hand there seems to be no doubt that this technique was used as a basis for the highly intricate etching found on fine-quality armours, notably the ones worn by German Protestants around 1560. These were decorated with deeply undercut scenes that appeared to float against their blackened background.

Damascening

This process involved inlaying fine strands of gold or silver in steel.

The preparation for damascening consisted of engraving the design directly onto the metal, which had previously been annealed in a fire-chamber. The incised channel had to be two-thirds of the diameter of the strand, which was inlaid by means of a cold chisel. The strand of precious metal was sunk in the prepared groove with a *matoir*, a tool used for dulling the surface of gold or silver and ensuring that it was firmly inlaid. The surface of the inlay was then burnished with a smooth file to reduce it to the level of the steel background. The art of damascening was only introduced into France during the 16th

century. Damascening could also be done in high relief – at an exorbitant price, of course. For this the raised parts of precious metal were handed over to the engraver, who then worked them, or rather sculpted them. This method produced a relief design instead of the completely flat, plane surface obtained by ordinary damascening.

Chiselling

The extremely difficult technique of chiselling was raised to the peak of its perfection by Italian sculptors. Benvenuto Cellini, in particular, has never been surpassed in the art.

ARMOUR (IV)
1. 1500. 2. Louis XII on the occasion of his entry into Genoa in 1507. The 'Father of his people' failed to live up to his own motto REX NON UTITUR ACULEO (The king has no goad) by committing terrible atrocities while he was in Italy. His actual armorial bearings are shown on page 76. The mane of his horse has been completely shaved off and its ears have been shortened to make it appear more frightening. This practice was already current in the reign of Charles VIII at the end of the previous century.

3. Maximilian armour (1510). 4. French gendarme (1510). The horse bards were probably made of cuir bouilli, according to the Italian fashion. The same applies to fig. 2. The celebrated Chevalier Bayard must have presented a somewhat similar appearance. 5. 1514. 6. 1532. The helmet is a burgonet with buffe. 7. 1537. 8. 1539. 9. 1540. The horse armour has a tailguard protecting the base of the spine; it is particularly conspicuous here and in fig. 11. The knight in this figure, and in the two following ones, would have worn a burgonet in action. 10. 1545. The crupper has been replaced by leather straps reinforced with 'fichures' (overlapping metal scales). 11. 1545. The horse armour has fichures, as in fig. 10. 12. 1560.

After 1550 bards tended to be limited to the chanfron and the shield of the peytral. They were to remain in use, however, until the reign of Louis XIII, who in 1628 entered La Rochelle wearing full armour with horse bards similar to those shown in fig. 1. Note the continuing use of the armet with half-visor worn in figs. 5 and 12 (see Part 1, pp. 38 and 40).

All the horses illustrated here are going at a walk apart from the last six, which are amblers, i.e., they are using the gait known as the amble, which is much less tiring for the rider (see Part 1, p. 50, fig. 2).

There must have been hundreds of tricks and knacks to successful chiselling, and all of them were jealously guarded by the superb craftsmen of Italy. Nevertheless, we can still detect a fair number of short cuts and subterfuges, some of them less reprehensible than others, behind their undeniable virtuosity. Moulding and *cire perdu*, for instance, must undoubtedly have played a large part in the production of many of these staggeringly beautiful creations.

Niello

This form of decoration involved inlaying, under heat, fine threads of black enamel composed of galenite, natural sulphur and lead. There were several imitations of niello in common use; these were cold-enamelled in black, red and white.

Gilding

Although armours made of solid silver did exist, it was generally considered sufficient to plate the finest suits with gold. Alternatively they could be gilded, either with gold-leaf or simply with a layer of powdered gold applied with a paintbrush.

Damascus steel

Damask, which is often confused with damascening, was a type of steel made exclusively in the East. It was used to make weapons, known as 'damasked' weapons, that combined flexibility with amazing toughness. They were decorated with designs that had a watered-silk appearance.

Embossing

The technique of embossing, which is often confused with chiselling, involved hammering out a pattern in relief. This process, which the Italians excelled at, was frequently used in conjunction with damascening; it was finished off with a small chisel.

A brief summary of the different techniques of applied decoration

1510 to 1530 Costume armour with chiselled bands of openwork. Fluting accompanied by etched designs.

1550 First embossed armours made at Augsburg.

1555 Floating, free style of decoration first introduced in Germany. Decoration consisting of

BALDRICS
In the Middle Ages the baldric was worn on the right hip and hung diagonally across the left thigh.

1 and 2. Mid 12th century. 3 and 4. Late 12th century. 5 and 6. Early 13th century. 7. 1250. 8 and 9. 1277. 10. 1280 (see note below). 11. Late 13th century. 12. Second half of 13th century. 13 and 14. 1300. 15–17. 1320. 18. 1325. 19 and 20. 1327. 21. 1360. 22. 1380. 23. 1400. 24. 1410. 25. 1420. 26. 1467. 27. 1472. 28. 1499. 29. 1490. 30. 15th century. 31. 1500. 32–34. 1530. 35 and 36. 1560. 37. 1578. 38 and 39. 1580. 40. 1585. 41. 1587. 42 and 43. 1590. 44 and 45. 1600.

The scabbards in figs. 5, 7, 8, 9, 12, 14, 15, 16, 19, 20 and 21 broaden out at the top in a metal ferrule known as a chape. Sometimes a 'sword-hat' or capule (figs. 10 and 18) were used to prevent rain from entering the scabbard. The decorative band at the top of the scabbard was known as a 'coipel' (see figs. 9, 16, 18, 19 and 20). The straps used to fasten the scabbard to the belt in figs. 22, 23, 24, 26, 27, 28, 29, 31 and 34 were called 'échalles', as were the chains shown in fig. 30; however, those in the following figures were known as 'hangers'.

16TH-CENTURY CAVALRY AND STANDARDS
(pp. 76–77)
1. Henri II of France in the uniform of a captain of Chevaulégers (*c.*1550). 2. The Emperor Charles V wearing half-armour (1547). 3. Trumpeter (*c.*1580). The colours of his uniform were the same as the livery of his captain and so varied constantly. 4. Armour (second half of 16th century). 5. Armour (1580).

Standards: 6. Standard of Louis XII (1498–1515). 7. Standard of Ivan the Terrible (1533–1548). 8. Standard of Charles V, emperor from 1519 onwards. 9. Standard of Charles V when he was still Charles I of Spain (1516). 10. Great standard of Spain in the 16th century, bearing the castle of Castile, the red lion of Leon, the black eagle of Sicily, the stripes of Aragon, the red eagle of Tyrol and the coat-of-arms of Burgundy. 11. Standard of the hereditary Prussian duchy of Poland, *c.*1600, with the Prussian eagle and the Polish eagle (the eagle of Prussia is on the back). 12. German cavalry standard (Palatinate-Deux-Ponts) 1569. 13. Huguenot standard during the Wars of Religion (1562). 14. Standard of Pope Julian II, who was famed for his battles against the Venetians and the French (1445–1513).

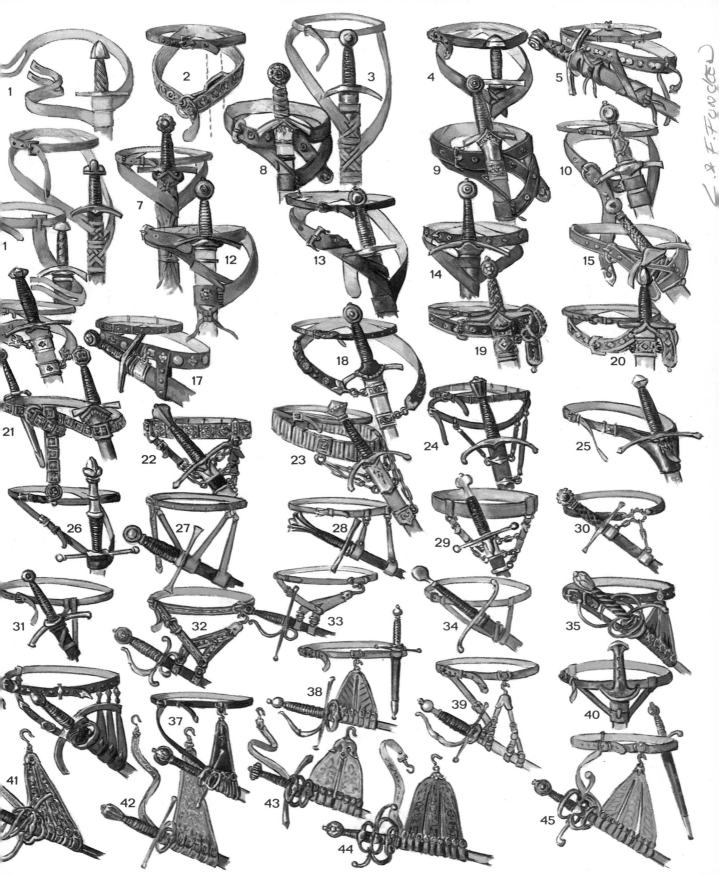

bands of different-coloured enamels (modelled on designs used in oriental carpets) in vogue in Poland, Lithuania, and Hungary. Etched and damascened vertical bands gradually replaced by intertwined bands.

1560 to 1570   Narrow diagonal bands in imitation of 'guilloche' fabric introduced in France.

1575   Vertical bands alternate with decorative motifs on Italian armours.

1580   Embossing and damascening reach their zenith in Italy.

1600   Milan introduces decoration in the form of large oval medallions. Mechanical techniques first used in embossing and etching.

One final rather interesting point concerns the methods used to store these magnificent armours while they were not in use. In the mid-15th century the usual practice was to store the suits on actual models in the armoury. Some rulers, such as Philip of Spain, even had a close likeness of their head made out of cast silver and painted in oils in lifelike colours. Heads like this are very rarely found nowadays.

Missing armours

The number of armours to be found in museums and private collections today is considerable, even though most of the pieces date from the 16th century. There is no question, however, that a huge quantity of these harnesses have been lost to us for ever. And the reasons for this are not simply time, rust and war.

Of course, we find our ancestors' lack of respect for outdated armours disappointing, yet at the same time it is perfectly understandable. They salvaged what they could of the metal; for example, plackarts were usually made into bucklers. The willful acts of vandalism carried out by heretics during the Wars of Religion, and, closer to our own times, in the French Revolution,[1] are distressing in quite a different way. As a result of these acts of destruction some armours that were in very good condition were

thrown onto the scrapheap, even though the only thing wrong with them was that they had been used to clothe a member of the hated aristocracy. Sons sold off cabinets full of magnificent pieces at dirt cheap prices; this is what happened to the collection of Marshal Strozzi in 1558. Brantôme watched 'with grief in his heart' as it was sold off at a tenth of its value.

Closer to our own times, at the beginning of the last century, armours were often lent out to painters or theatre producers. In London cuirasses were even unearthed from the Tower of London (which was, after all, a kind of arsenal) to equip the Royal Horse guards in 1821. The halberdiers of the Lord Mayor's escort wore relics borrowed from the Tower until 1877, and the 'legs' from a foot-combat armour belonging to Henry VIII (a superb example of Missaglia's craftsmanship, incidentally) were only recovered in 1947 – mouldering in a castle in Lincolnshire.

OFFICERS AT THE END OF THE 16TH CENTURY
1. Henri, Duke of Guise, in the uniform of an infantry general (1580). 2. François de Montmorency, marshal of France (1576). Note the medial ridge of his breastplate, terminating in a prominent point at the lower end. This was an imitation of the civilian doublet of the period (fig. 2). This point was to continue to lengthen until it resembled an overhanging hump in shape (fig. 1). It was known as a peascod breastplate in England and a *Gansbauch* (literally, goose belly) in Germany. Note also that the armour in fig. 1. has no couters or lower cannons.

3. General (1580). The term 'general' was used for the first time in the writings of Brantôme (1540–1614). The ruff worn by the general in the picture was irreverently nicknamed a 'St John's platter' in reference to the Biblical martyr who was beheaded. The ruff had in fact been worn by men since 1576, but during the reign of Henri III it grew to an impressively large size (as shown here). 4. Infantry officer with his page (1572). 5. Infantry officer (1580). 6. Infantry officer (1590).

7. Standard of Charles IX (1560–1574). 8. Standard of Henri III (1574–1589). 9. Standard of Henri IV (1589–1610).

---

[1] The reason we do not know the names of the master-armourers of France is because the precious archives containing details of their identity were totally destroyed during the French Revolution.

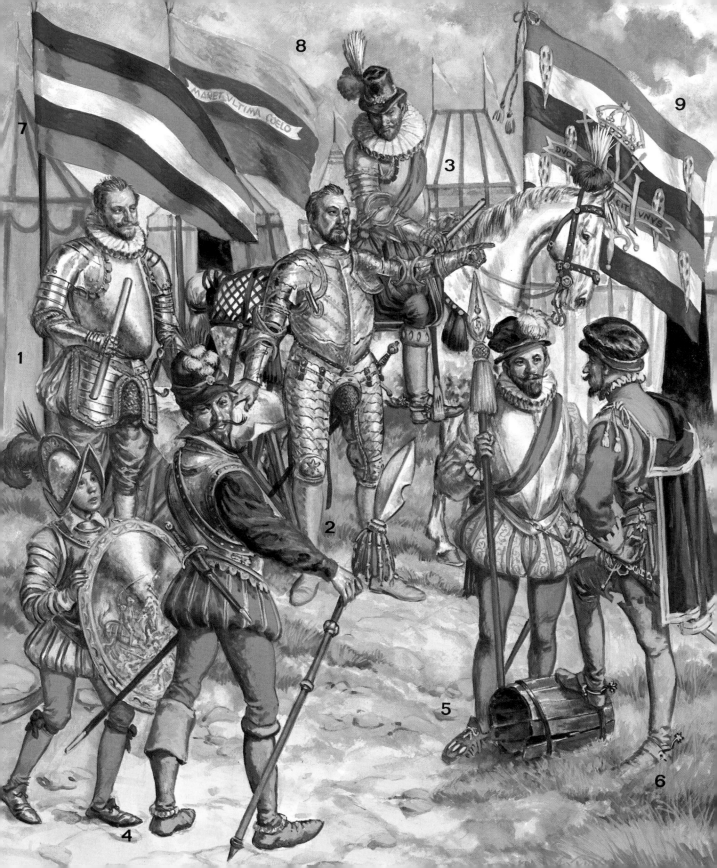

The scarf

Fighting men wore a succession of garments that bore some means of identifying the wearer: first, the surcoat emblazoned with a coat-of-arms or cross in the colours of the individual nation; next, the aketon, the arming doublet, and the tabard; and lastly, the mandilla. However, with the introduction of the scarf – a more obvious badge of identity – applied decoration on armour no longer had to be hidden by an overgarment. In France, men-at-arms wore a white or black scarf, depending on whether they belonged to the Catholic or Protestant party. A green or isabel (light tan) colour could also be used. Both the English and the Savoyards wore a blue scarf, the Spaniards wore a red one, the Austrians a black and yellow one, and the Dutch an orange one.

According to some sources the scarf was adopted because it meant that men-at-arms, who were in the habit of discarding bits of their armour from time to time, could no longer conceal missing pieces under an overgarment. This idea is frequently brought up in writings on the subject, but we regard it as an obvious fallacy which we do not subscribe to at all.

The much-quoted opinion of La Noue,[1] who was a brave man and a gallant captain, states that gentlemen 'went to such extremes that the majority of them weighed themselves down with anvils instead of covering themselves in armour'. Perhaps La Noue is like Clausewitz, however, in that everyone quotes him but nobody reads him.[2] What La Noue actually wrote in the fifteenth of his *Discours politiques et militaires* was (and we quote verbatim): 'Now because of the power of arquebusses and pikes they were right to make harnesses stronger and more proof against weapons than before. However they went to such extremes that . . .' etc., etc. Here we have a good illustration of the justifiable concern of fighting men to protect themselves, rather than risk exposing themselves to certain death for the supposed sake of physical comfort. It should be added, however, that the very few armours weighing between 45 and 54 kilograms that have survived to the present day are in fact siege armours – virtual blockhouses designed to protect famous personages who wanted to 'visit the trenches'.

Armour was only completely abandoned in the reign of Louis XIII, when the ultimate failure of the cuirass to meet the challenge from the increasing power of the bullet was finally recognized.

[1] Francois de la Noue (1531–1591), known as Bras de Fer, became a convert to the Reformation at the age of twenty-seven. He fought on the side of Condé's troops, where his chivalrous conduct in battle earned him the nickname of the 'Huguenot Bayard'. In 1570 his left hand was amputated as a result of an injury from an arquebus ball. Thereafter he wore a jointed artificial limb that was ultimately responsible for causing his death. One day during an assault, as he clung, still stunned by a round of arquebus fire, to the top of a siege ladder, his 'hand' came apart! La Noue survived all the political upheavals of his day to serve Henri II, Charles IX, Henri de Navarre, Henri III (who made him a marshal of France), and lastly, Henri IV. He was captured and imprisoned by the Spanish in 1579, but he turned his five harsh years of captivity to good account by writing the bulk of his *Discours*. This work, written in a graphic style, constitutes one of the most valuable documents of 16th-century French in existence today.

[2] These remarks by la Noue are often wrongly attributed to R.P. Daniel, who appropriated them in his *Histoire de la milice Française*, published in 1724.

ARMOUR IN THE 16TH CENTURY
1. Armour belonging to Henri II (*c*.1545). Note the greaves covering the shins, which have been made thinner for the sake of lightness (this was a common and fairly obvious thing to do in the case of 'lobster'-style cuisses). Henri II was an enthusiastic collector of *de luxe* armours. The one shown here is jointed above the waist after the fashion of 'animes', or fully laminated breastplates. Their so-called flexibility was in fact limited to the abdominal area. 2. Italian armour (mid-16th century). It has a matching burgonet with a bevor or buffe similar to the one shown in fig. 1. An optional traditional-style armet also came with the suit. 3. Armour of the Duke of Cumberland (*c*.1590). The fleur-de-lys and the rose are emblems of Elizabeth I (Cumberland was her 'champion'). 4. King Henri IV in 1596. The broad-brimmed felt hat he is wearing was the classic headgear for men. Plumes were worn exclusively by military leaders during the Wars of Religion; in fact there were even some generals who were not permitted to wear them. 5. Captain of the infantry bodyguard of the 'Enfants d'honneur'. This corps was made up of former pages who had grown up with the prince. 6. Italian armour with its characteristic 'Savoyard' helmet (*c*.1600). On the ground beside it is another model of a Savoyard mask helmet dating from the same period. These armours were used to equip the troops of Charles Emmanuel of Savoy, who were defeated outside Geneva in 1602.

The majority of ordinary armours were now left unpolished. Instead they were coated with brown or black varnish so as to do away with the need for constant care and maintenance.

III THE ROLE OF ARTILLERY IN THE DEVELOPMENT OF TACTICS

Tactics

Over the years the knight on horseback gradually perfected his basic military tactic, which consisted of a shock cavalry charge in which he threw all the speed of his galloping mount behind the force of his lance. We have seen in preceding chapters how both the offensive and defensive weapons of the knight became progressively more heavy with time.

The infantry, with its *péquins* (pikemen) and shot, played only a very secondary role at this stage. It was mainly used to worry the enemy flanks or to form a line behind which the cavalry could reform after charging. So far only the English had begun to realize the true military potential of a strong infantry. On the continent, on the other hand, the brilliant victory won at Woeringen[1] by a combined cavalry and infantry operation did nothing to change the contemptuous attitude of the feudal lords towards footsoldiers – especially in France, where warfare continued to be regarded as the prerogative of the knighthood. By persisting in this attitude they simply gave the rank and file of the commoners an excuse to claim ever greater rewards for the services they gave in battle.

The medieval knight was to institute the humane practice of ransoming prisoners. However, this turned out to have a disastrous effect on the crude tactics that had hitherto been employed. Henceforth the knight and his 'lance' would desert the banner and rush off to try to capture the most richly-dressed member of the enemy they could lay hands on. Woe betide any opponent who was wounded but not ransomable!

Even Joan of Arc was unable to stop the slaughter, and one English prisoner she tried to protect

was ruthlessly finished off despite her intervention. However, cruelty and greed were not restricted to any one particular class. The rank and file were often the first to disband to go and plunder an enemy camp or take part in the many massacres and burnings that chequer the history of the Hundred Years' War.

And yet this contemptible infantry was eventually to succeed in withstanding and defeating the hitherto invincible might of the cavalry. First the commoners, then the English archers at Crécy, Poitiers, and Agincourt,[2] and finally the Swiss succeeded in winning the grudging respect of their proud adversaries – so much so, in fact, that the cavalry tried to beat them at their own game by dismounting and shortening their lances. What an unlikely infantry those knights must have made, weighed down by their suits of full armour.

TACTICS (I)
1a. Old formation (late 15th–early 16th centuries) grouping together four types of combatant (see figurines and colour-code below). 1b. 'Battle' in defensive position against an attack on its right wing. This formation comprised 180 arquebusiers, 190 archers, 342 pikemen, and 294 halberdiers. 2a. 'New' formation made up of two types of combatant (324 arquebusiers and 1,108 pikemen). The 'battle' is shown in marching order during action. 2b. Deployment in stationary battle order. Reverse manoeuvres were carried out to get back into marching order. 3. Types of combatants (early 16th century); the colour of their plinths corresponds to the diagrams in figs. 1, 2 and 4: a) arquebusier; b) archer or arbalester; c) pikeman carrying 5.85 metre pike; d) halberdier. The sword-and-buckler men armed with two-hand swords are not represented here. They were optional combatants, and usually in a minority. They normally stood in the middle of the halberdiers (see following plate). 4. A 'battle' of six companies in action. Four companies of pikemen (420 men) and two companies of arquebusiers (210 men) drawn up: a) in marching order in echelon; b) in battle order; c) in a defensive formation to prevent encirclement.

[1] See Part I, p. 46.
[2] See Part I, pp. 77 and 88.

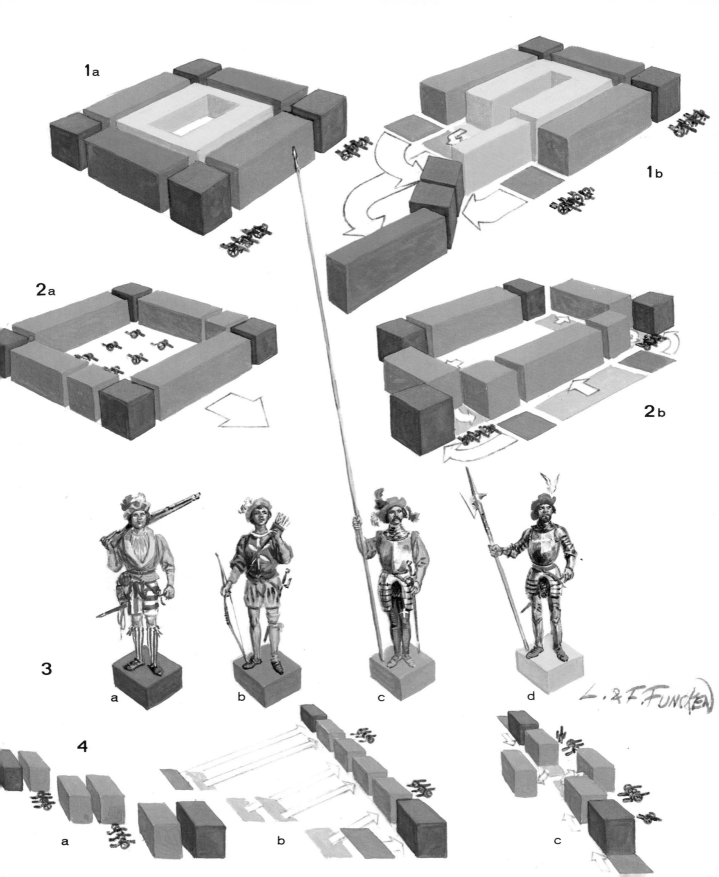

1a

1b

2a

2b

3

a b c d

L. & F. FUNCKEN

4

a b c

About the same period the Hussite troops of Jan Zizka[1] in Bohemia introduced the novel tactic of using a barrier of covered wagons[2] drawn up in square formation. For five successive crusades cavalry charges broke against the wall of these wagons to no avail. The ranks of the attackers were first shattered by hand-gun fire, then engaged in hand-to-hand combat by the infantry, who sprang out from behind the safety of their wagons. Zizka's successors, the brothers Procope, carried on fighting for ten more years. It was total war, waged fiercely on both sides. The Hussites would go into battle singing the hymn written by the leader – incidentally one of the finest Bohemian songs of the 15th century. It began with the words, 'You, champions, who uphold the eternal laws of God . . .' Unfortunately these fine sentiments did not prevent the massacre of 15,000 monks and the destruction of 600 Roman Catholic buildings within ten years.

The 'fortified wagon' idea was also adopted in Germany, where a modified version of it was used on occasions. This involved hanging a thick plank with loopholes pierced in it between the four wheels of the wagon. However the rapid rise of artillery led to the eventual abandonment of the *Wagenburg* around 1560.

In 1513 a French engineer came up with the idea of a fortified camp in separate pieces. It was to be connected together by hinges and defended by a hundred arquebusses-à-croc; however, the high cost and time needed to erect it meant that this particular project was never put into practice.

The tactics that eventually won the day were those used by the Swiss, in which the offensive was the all-important thing. (We have already seen how effective their methods were in practice.[3] Before the advent of the Swiss there was only one French military leader who exploited his infantry to the full, namely du Guesclin. He waged a 'good hard' fight, but his methods were far from being popular with his fellow knights.[4] Nevertheless the obstinate Breton did have his disciples, among them Poton de Xaintrailles, La Hire, and Dunois. After his death military art in France simply went into a decline, and the army was afraid even to confront the English in open battle.

The first French field artillery appeared suddenly on the battlefield and completely overturned the hitherto invincible strategy of the invading English armies. The enemy front line was thrown into disarray by a violent initial assault by the artillery, and in the ensuing disorder a breach was opened up into which footsoldiers and cavalry rushed. The English knights of the late King Henry V protested 'This is not war!' Thus cannon introduced a new tactic into war. Although it still only counted as a back-up weapon, its reputation continued to grow, and because of it the French army invading Italy under Charles VIII was seen as an 'object of terror'.

The nobility continued to fight on horseback as this symbolised its traditional status. However,

[1] Jan de Trokov, nicknamed Zizka (the one-eyed), 1380–1424. He took over command of the Taborite sect who rebelled against the rule of the Roman Catholic church following the martyrdom of Han Huss. Before he succumbed to the plague, Zizka ordered that a drum should be made out of his skin. Frederick the Great was reputed to have taken delivery of it 'among the spoils brought back from Bohemia'. Voltaire wrote to his famous patron on the 16th November, 1743:

> Is it true that in your court
> You have placed, this autumn
> Among the furnishings of the Crown
> The skin of this famous drum
> That Zizka had made of his skin?

This drum was also mentioned in Bruckmann's *Epistolae itinerariae*. It may seem surprising, but this macabre and barbarous practice was not at all unusual. The Taborites' emblem of a chalice striking the standards (see Part 2, p. 49) earned them the nickname of 'soldiers of the chalice'.

[2] The Hussite armies had as many as 500 of these wagons in 1426.

[3] See the chapter on the Swiss, Part 2, p. 60.

[4] See Volume I, p. 26, caption 11.

TACTICS (II)

1. Tactics used by pikemen against cavalry. The Swiss infantry was the first to adopt the long pike that was capable of stopping an armoured cavalry charge. The pikes' target was the actual horses; unseated riders were attacked by halberdiers who rushed in as a second wave. 2. Tactics used by sword-and-buckler men and halberdiers. The Swiss excelled at the massed charge against stationary enemy infantry. After the first attack, pikes were virtually useless because they were so long, so the sword-and-buckler men and halberdiers were immediately brought in. They moved between the pikes to cut down the front ranks of the opposing pikemen, thereby causing disarray in the enemy 'battle'. 3. Tactics used by arquebusiers. A file twelve men deep would provide continuous fire: a fires while b gets ready to take his place; a moves to the back of the line to reload, and b takes his place and fires; meanwhile the ten remaining arquebusiers all move up one place. The other files that make up the company would carry out the same movements simultaneously. 4. Triangular battle order adopted by an isolated body of troops who do not know which direction the enemy are planning to attack from.

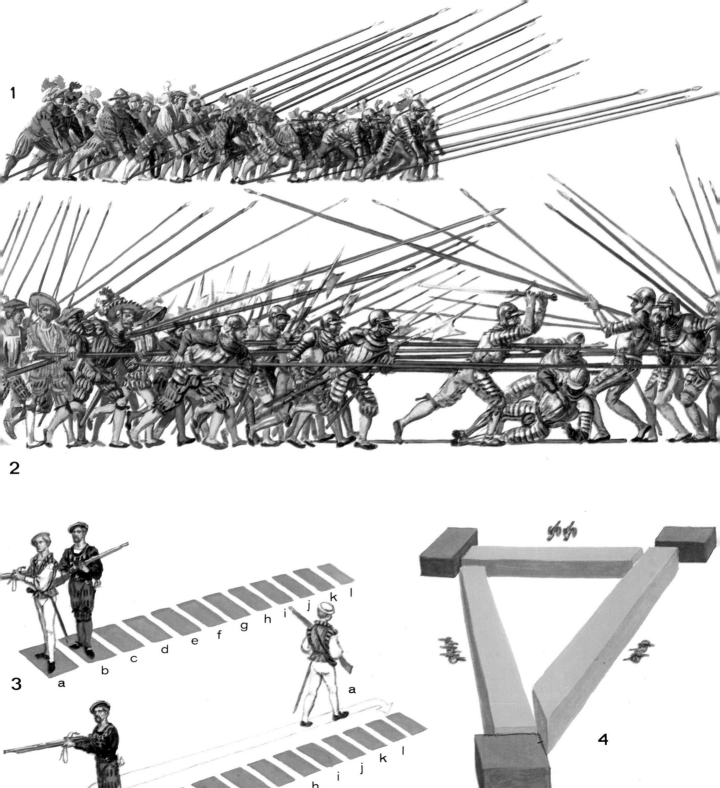

regular national infantries modelled on Swiss lines were growing up all over Europe. The new infantry adopted the deadly arquebus, using it indiscriminately, without any regard for the old rules and standards of war, to massacre the gendarmerie. Their impact, meanwhile, was growing less effective with each day that passed. The infantryman was no longer addressed by the contemptuous names of 'lackey', 'lout', or 'rogue'; henceforth he was called 'soldier' – a telling indication of his new status.

[1] *Coronelias* (from *coronel*, a colonel) meant a unit made up of twelve companies.

In Spain the tactical unit called the 'tercio' was introduced. The name 'tercio' is derived either from the 3,000 men that initially went to make up its full strength, or from the three *coronelias*, or *corunelas*,[1] that formed the actual square formation. Another possibility is that the word is a reference to the three types of soldier fighting in this unit, namely pikemen, sword-and-buckler men, and arquebusiers. These regiments were the means of Spanish domination in Europe until the mid-17th century.

Brantôme has left us a particularly vivid description of the new 'musketeers' making their first

TACTICS (III)

1. 'Battle' drawn up in attacking formation. It could attack at the same time as defending itself on all sides by adopting a 'hedgehog' formation. The military tactics of the Swiss spread to the rest of Europe, and were applied with varying degrees of success from the late 15th century onwards. In the 16th century Spanish infantry gained a remarkable reputation for bravery and discipline. (The different colours correspond to the following types of soldier: red: arquebusiers, yellow: halberdiers; blue: pikemen). 2. A Spanish *tercio* in marching order (in 1602 the term *tercio* was extended to cover the Dutch regiments in the service of Spain). This is one of 'those great battalions in close formation that resembled so many towers, only the towers were able to repair the breaches made in them' – this is how the great French writer Bossuet was to describe the *tercio* a little later.

3. A 'lance' of the bandes d'ordonnance in 1545: A) the gendarme or leader of the lance; B) the squire (optional) wearing a laminated cuirass called an 'anime'; C) the page; D) the coutillier; E) the three archers (sometimes only two were used). The names coutillier and archer were in fact very old and originally referred to a man-at-arms and a Chevau-léger. Helmets and horse bards were worn during marches by packhorses and their riders. The footsoldiers who formed part of the lance had been done away with in 1506. In 1522 Charles V fixed the strength of the gendarmerie at eight companies, each containing fifty 'lances'. The number of companies was raised to nineteen in 1545, but fell to fifteen again in 1547. In wartime a large number of temporary bands were raised; these were known as the new ('nouvelles') bands or the supplementary bands ('bandes de crue'). The lances in fig. 3 are being held in raised position, when they were said to be 'uncovered' or 'manifest'. The page is carrying a small lance called a 'genette'. 4 and 5. Lancers from a bande d'ordonnance in 1572. The discarding of leg-harness made it possible to reinforce the cuirass against bullets. The mandilla with loose sleeves is typical of the period between 1570 and 1580. The lancer on the left has his lance lowered; when it was held in this position it was said to be 'trailed' or 'hidden', 'secret', or 'covered'. By adopting this position the rider hoped to trick the enemy and make him 'feel the thrust of the lance' when he was too close in to break off fighting.

ARTILLERY (I); MID-16TH CENTURY (pp. 88–89)
View of a siege artillery emplacement protected by gabions; the illustration is based on an aquarelle from the *Recueil du règlement général de l'ordre et conduite de l'artillerie* (*Anthology of regulations concerning the organization and conduct of artillery*) by Captain Bénédict de Vasselieu, known as Nicolas Lyonnais. Although this work is dated 1613, it was in fact written during the reign of Henri III (1574–1589) and depicts actual artillery used in the reign of Henri II (1547–1559).

1. Laying a cannon. The master-gunner is shielded by a special board (see fig. 4) to protect him from enemy look-out fire. 2. Firing the cannon. 3. Preparing the cannon for firing. A gunner is cleaning out the cannon with a swab while the rest of the team get the powder charge ready. 4. Gun-layer's protective shield (see fig. 1). 5. Hurdle holding the cannon in position on its platform while it is being loaded. 6. Tuft of grass that acts as wad for the powder and ball. 7. Hole in the ground used to store the gunpowder. 8. Shelter for storing stocks of gunpowder. 9. Elite arquebusiers detailed to 'cover' the chief gunner while he is laying the cannon. Contrary to the usual practice, they are wearing bullet-proof cuirasses owing to the highly dangerous nature of their assignment. They wore neutral-coloured uniforms and unpolished helmets and cuirasses to make them less conspicuous. 10. Mortar in position for firing. 11. Staff weapons to be used in the event of an enemy raid.

(*Inset*) Embrasures found in 16th-century fortifications: 12. Redan and beak. 13. So-called 'French' embrasure. 14. Redan. 15. 'Swivel' embrasure. The various redans, tiers, and projections were supposed to stop enemy projectiles which might otherwise have ricocheted and entered the funnel-shaped embrasures. The 'swivel' type of defence, which was very rare, enabled the defender to shoot in any direction while having maximum protection from enemy fire – particularly as he could close his embrasure by rotating the swivel through a half-turn in between firing.

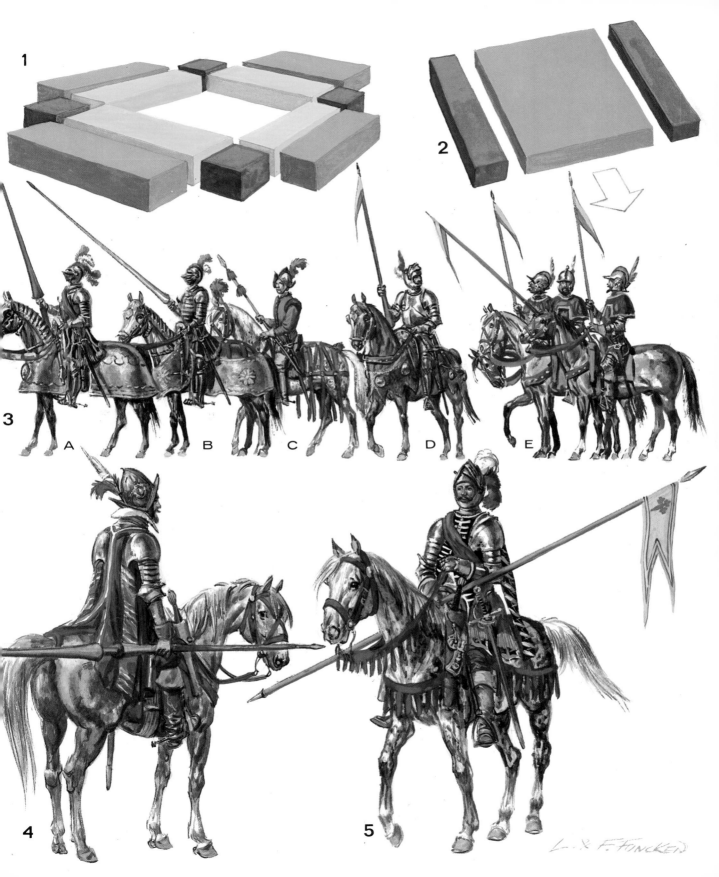

1

2

3

A   B   C   D   E

4   5

L. & F. Fiincken

appearance in 1567: 'those who carried them [muskets] were called musketeers; they were very well paid and respected, to the extent of having big tall churls to carry their weapons across country for them. However, when they were on sentry duty, or marched in battle order, or went on guard, or entered a town, then the 'musketeers' took back their weapons. You would have thought they were princes to see them, they were so haughty and marched so arrogantly, with such fine airs; and whenever there was a battle or skirmish you could hear these words shouted in deference to them: 'Salgan, salgan los mosqueteros! afuera, afuera, adelante los mosqueteros!' All of a sudden people would make way for them; they were even more respected than captains at that time because they were new, and novelty always pleases'.

The square or rectangle that made up the 'hedgehog' formation adopted by the tercios at times numbered up to 8,000 men; arquebusiers tended to account for an increasing proportion of this strength. The men were trained to co-ordinate their movements and action with those of adjoining battalions. Strategy tended to consist of manoeuvres, interspersed with long hours of observing the enemy. Full-scale battles were rare, and war continued to be, according to Montluc,[1] 'simply a matter of fights, encounters, skirmishes, and ambushes.'

The Duke of Alba and Alessandro Farnese relied on delaying tactics of a similar nature which were to make no impact at all on the art of war. However, they did succeed in achieving their objectives by dint of subtle manoeuvring. They managed to exhaust and disrupt mercenary armies who had no sense of loyalty to a cause to sustain them; they also isolated and captured fortified towns by a clever stratagem that involved cutting off enemy supply lines.

In 1590 Maurice of Nassau, Prince of Orange, was appointed chief of the Dutch armies at the age of twenty-three; he was to become recognized as the most brilliant strategist of his day. Taking as his model the Roman maniple, he confronted the formidable massed ranks of the Spanish tercios with a formation three lines deep drawn up in chequer-board fashion. He did away with the heavy tactics inherited from the Swiss, and in their place introduced a new lightness and mobility, indispensable for carrying out rapid evolutions. His other innovation was the relieving of battle-weary troops, which made possible a more sustained action and a more economical deployment of troops. His army was to become the training-ground for the regiments of both England and France, and many future great commanders, among them Turenne, were disciples of the great Dutch military leader.

Artillery

In Part 2 we saw the various stages by which the early bombards of the 14th century were removed from the primitive wooden troughs they rested on. The lighter guns were then mounted on wheeled gun-carriages, and hence, by the mid-15th century, they came to acquire the characteristic outlines of the modern cannon. However, this vital step forward in the progress of the cannon towards full mobility had not yet been instituted by the time that the new weapon was first used on the battlefield at Crécy, in 1346. Such, at any rate, is the generally accepted date, although the source for this piece of information, Froissart the chronicler, was only eight or nine years old at the time. Not surprisingly, perhaps, his account has been vigorously challenged by some authorities. It would be even more presumptuous to claim that the two or three cannon used on this occasion played any kind of decisive role in the battle.

Be that as it may, England was, along with Italy, probably one of the first countries to use field artillery and to fire the metal cannonballs known as 'plummets'. These came into general use from the mid-14th century onwards.

ARTILLERY (II)
Gun-laying could either be carried out scientifically, with the aid of a quadrant (figs. 1 and 3), or by using guesswork and a graduated rule (fig. 2). Many gunners simply relied on using their eye and the judgement they had gained with long experience. The three cannons shown in the illustration date from the beginning of the 16th century.

---

[1] Blaise de Montluc, military historian (1507–1577). His career as a soldier lasted for fifty-five years, during which time he received twenty-four wounds in the course of five battles, seventeen assaults, eleven sieges, and two hundred fights and skirmishes.

1

2

3

Light artillery consisting of ribaldequins or multiple guns firing several barrels simultaneously was known to exist in Bruges from 1339 onwards. These small cannon were very probably brought over from the continent by Edward III. It has to be admitted, however, that field artillery was of little more than curiosity value in the 14th century and had no significant effect on the course of countless battles of the period.

Siege artillery, on the other hand, was quite a different proposition. It served as a powerful instrument in the consolidation of the power of the monarch, as even the stoutest castle walls of rebellious feudal lords were unable to withstand it. Although this heavy artillery was still fairly primitive, it could still open up terrible breaches in curtain walls, and it rapidly led to the disappearance of traditional siege engines – the last assault-tower on wheels was used in battle in 1356, in France. However, the long career of these old ballistic engines continued until the middle of the following century at least. They were used in conjunction with the excellent artillery of the Bureau brothers, and between 1449 and 1450 they made possible the recapture of sixty fortifications in sixteen months.

The oldest known French treatise on artillery was written just prior to this, in 1430, and bore the evocative title of *Livre du secret de l'art de l'artillerie et cannonerie* (*Book on the secrets of the art of artillery and cannonry*). However, the oldest manual in existence had been written in German nearly eighty years previously: it was entitled *Die Anleitung Schiesspulver zu bereiten, Büchsen zu laden und zu beschiessen* (*Method for preparing powder and loading and firing cannon*).

French artillery in the 15th century was probably the best equipped and the best organized of its day. The excellent deployment and skilful exploitation of its potential shown by the Bureau brothers and Pierre Bessoneau, 'master-general and inspector of the King's artillery', revolutionized the tactics used in battles and sieges. Their methods halted the hitherto irresistible force of the cavalry charge;[1] they shattered the ranks of the formidable English archers and instituted techniques of modern siege warfare, including batteries protected by barrels filled with earth, communication trenches, and ammunition depots. However, far away to the East another formidable infantry, this time belonging to Muhammed II, had in 1453 brought the massive walls of Constantinople crashing to the ground, and with them a centuries-old empire.

The wealthy Duke of Burgundy, Charles the Bold, made it 'a point of honour' to have at his disposal the largest and most powerful artillery in Europe. At Brusthem, in 1467, the Burgundian light artillery crushed 18,000 Liégois without the aid of cavalry. The Duke suffered a less happy fate against the Swiss infantry outside Granson, where he abandoned 419 guns of every type to the enemy. According to an already old-established custom, the biggest cannon each had individual names, and among the spoils at Granson were 'The Shepherd and The Shepherdess' and 'the Four Sisters'.

The field carriages of the Burgundian artillery were remarkably advanced for their day and had an ingenious system for aiming the guns.[2] The heavy guns were transported on four-wheeled carriages, or hung by ropes beneath the axles of the carts that were used to winch them onto their old-style stationary mountings.[3]

Elevation by means of trunnions (pivots on either side of the gun that supported it on its carriage) came into more widespread use around 1480. The principle behind trunnions, which in the past have been described as a 'cunning' and even an 'inspired' invention, had, as we have demonstrated, already been discovered as early as 1400. However, the idea

ARTILLERY (III)

1. Hand-gun (1505). In fact this was a very large arquebus-à-croc. The illustration shows the shooter leaning on the tripod stand with all his weight to counteract the force of the recoil. This stand has been ingeniously designed so that it can be dismantled into two parts. 2. Cannon with removable breechblock (c. 1570). It is still based on the same system used in the old veuglaire (see Part 2, p. 35, figs. 4 to 8), though the basic principle has undergone considerable refinement. This type of breechloading cannon was doomed to oblivion, however, and was to be superseded for several centuries by muzzle-loading guns. Despite the practicality of the method it had the serious disadvantage of allowing too much combustive gas to escape. On the right of fig. 2 is a diagram showing the breechblock in position with the cartridge of powder and the ball.

[1] John Talbot, the 'English Achilles', was killed by French artillery fire when he led a charge at the head of his knights outside Castillon in the Gironde, on 17 July, 1453. He was eighty years old.
[2] See Part 2, p. 37, figs. 4, 5 and 6.
[3] See Part 2, p. 37, figs, 1, 2 and 3.

1

2

A F. Funcken

could only be developed when advances in techniques of gun-making made it possible to cast on trunnions in one piece with the cannon itself. This advance meant that heavy guns no longer had to be loaded by means of a breechblock; now that they were removed from their old-fashioned fixed mountings there was nowhere to wedge the handy 'fire-box', or chamber, in position. In any case recent improvements in the manufacture of gunpowder tended to make it 'grainier' and far more powerful than before, and it would have blown up breechblocks. Hence the idea of manufacturing cannon in the shape of a tube closed at one end caught on very rapidly indeed, and this basic principle was to continue unchallenged for centuries until 1886.

Henceforth the cannon could be pivoted easily on its trunnions to allow it to be raised to the desired height and then wedged in position. However the rack-and-pinion method of adjusting the height of the barrel continued to be used for small- and medium-calibre guns alongside the other, more sophisticated methods shown in the illustrations.

The art of casting cannon had gained a new prominence in Germany since the first small-scale efforts produced at the end of the 14th century. However, in the Low Countries Flanders, Brabant, and the town of Dinant had been centres of gun-making for centuries.

The Burgundians, despite the strength of their artillery, were the first army in history to be on the receiving end of an artillery barrage. This took place outside Neuss in 1475, when they were fighting the imperial infantry of Frederick III of Hapsburg. In contrast Edward IV's planned invasion of France clearly shows that England was lagging behind its continental rivals in terms of artillery strength. In 1475 the Messenger brothers were still using guns with breechblocks that had to be transported on special carriages.

The Turks were the last to use giant cannon, which they often massed together in groups of twelve. A Hungarian founder called Orban cast the biggest gun of his day for Muhammed II in 1452: it was nearly 9 metres long and could fire a cannonball measuring 0.924 metres in diameter and weighing 450 kilos up to a range of 1600 metres.

In France the skill and experience of gunmakers like Simon enabled Charles VII to 'terrify Italy' with the sight of his 140 cannon, twelve of which were large-calibre. In 1507 his successor, Louis XII, took with him across the Alps sixty heavy cannon, 500 light guns and hackbuts, and a company of 720 gunners.

In Austria founding expanded rapidly under the impetus created by two skilled gunmakers from Innsbruck, Seelos and Endorfer. As a result several lavishly decorated cannon were produced after 1485, in the reign of Maximilian I. Production was increased considerably and this led to the setting up of the first modern arsenals. Bavaria and Brandenburg also had a powerful artillery at their disposal during the same period, and German artillery was undoubtedly the finest of its day.

Despite improvements made by his predecessors the Emperor Charles V found himself, in 1519, the owner of a vast array of guns of different calibres that were made from a variety of materials (cast iron, copper, bronze, and iron), and fired ammunition of stone, iron, and lead. The difficulties of supplying such a bewildering range of guns, and the many mistakes that must have occurred as a result, can well be imagined. Gunners, in fact, were reduced to marking each gun and cannonball separately with its own individual number. This extremely bizarre state of affairs can be explained by the fact that the various states that went to make up the vast Hapsburg empire each had their own artillery.

Charles V set about trying to standardize the calibre of his artillery, beginning with a decree to the effect that henceforth all guns were to be cast within his territories. The first experiments in standardization took place in Brussels, and eventually in 1535, after numerous attempts, the Spanish foundries of Malaga successfully turned out the first

ARTILLERY (IV)
1. System for elevation using a screw (1460). 2. Organ-serpentine (late 16th century). The triangular cylinder could revolve so that the thirty small guns could be fired off in succession. 3. Schrympe, or ribaldequin (1544). 4. Multi-barrelled gun showing the method used for elevation (16th century). 5. System allowing elevation in two possible positions as well as horizontal aiming (c.1500).

1

2

3

4

5

L. & Flynder

series of four standard types of cannon firing cast-iron balls weighing 1.3, 2.7, 18, and 36 kilos respectively. This measure was enforced throughout all the territories belonging to the Empire. Nevertheless it took until the end of the century before the old calibres, which were known as bastard-calibres, were completely eliminated. The ineffectiveness of giant cannon was demonstrated by Suleiman the Magnificent at the siege of Vienna in 1529, and subsequently production of them was abandoned for good. Belgian foundries especially were noted for the quality of their cannon. Malines, in particular, exported its products to Spain, Portugal, and England. Henry VIII ordered more than 140 cannon from the master gunmaker Hans Poppenruyter; among these were the famous Twelve Apostles which he used in his first campaign against France in 1511. Charles V also had his Twelve Apostles, which for a long time were regarded as models of their kind, and Louis XII of France owned twelve large cannon that were named after famous knights.

Francis I, the unfortunate adversary of Charles V, gave a decisive impetus to the organization of French artillery by increasing its strength and introducing a greater degree of standardization. During his reign French cannon were reduced to a mere eight calibres; Italy, by comparison, still had twenty-six in 1562.[1]

The upheavals of civil war prevented any new progress being made in the development of artillery

[1] Every Italian city had its own artillery – hence the range of different types of cannon.

ARTILLERY (V)
1. Gun positioned on a limber (a) with swingletrees for harnessing it to horses. It uses a rack-and-pinion method (b) of elevation, with a choice of nine different angles (c.1500). To fire the cannon the limber was removed and the trail of the carriage was allowed to rest on the ground, as shown in the diagram on the right. 2. Field-gun with limber and provision for elevation (1518). The masterly technique of Albrecht Dürer has captured every detail of the artillery of the period in his engravings. 3. Cannon that can be aimed vertically and horizontally by means of a screw (c.1520). It is a testimony to the inexhaustible inventiveness of military engineers of the period. Here the master-gunner is laying the gun with the maximum possible precision using a quarter circle fitted with a plumb-line. The expertise of these master-gunners was a combination of practical and theoretical knowledge, and meant they were much sought-after.

in France. In Germany, on the other hand, the new foundries at Heidenheim, Aschau, and Werfsten were in the process of introducing a whole range of technical improvements in their first-class products. Meanwhile the mathematician Hartmann of Nuremberg had devised an ingenious apparatus that could accurately estimate the weight of all types of cannonball (stone, iron, and lead) using the calibre of any cannon; it could also determine the exact amount of gunpowder required. The explosive detonating bomb had been introduced as early as 1550. It was fired by a mortar and exploded on contact with the ground, like the modern shell.

By the end of the century the leading nations of Europe had all restricted their artillery to a maximum of six or seven different calibres. These corresponded to the types of cannon listed below:

Type of cannon	Calibre (in cms)	Weight of ball (in kilos)	Weight of cannon (in kilos)
Heavy cannon	18	20	4,250
Cannon moyane	15	12	3,500
Great culverin	12	8	2,800
Bastard culverin	9	4	2,000
Culverin moyane	6	1.5	1,200
Falcon	4	0.5	600
Falconet	3	0.35	400
Mortar	35	50	3,000

1

b

a

2

L.&F.
FUNCKEN

3

The aim of this synoptic table is simply to give a rough idea of the common characteristics of artillery in the second half of the 16th century. The problems of conversion were not made any easier by old pounds, which tend to vary in weights from one city to another. It should also be noted that the weight of a solid iron cannonball and a lead ball can differ by up to a third, while the hollow iron ball filled with lead falls somewhere in between the two.

Ammunition

One of the most unusual missiles ever fired into the air must have been the square 'ball' made in 1346 by an iron founder in Bruges.

The more conventional stone ball was used in vast quantities for all types of cannon, despite its unfortunate tendency to crumble on impact when fired at walls. After 1350 its place was taken by the iron ball, though small-calibre lead ball had already been introduced several years before. At the end of the 15th century bronze began to be used in the manufacture of cannonballs; it lasted until the reign of Henri IV, although it obviously cost far more than cast iron. Balls were also made out of stone covered in lead or banded in iron – in fact, because of its cheapness, stone was never entirely abandoned. There were all kinds of new missiles dreamt up – for example, reamed balls linked together by a chain or bar, and incendiary balls that were heated to incandescence or filled with some inflammable substance. Lastly, light artillery would sometimes fire a volley of case shot at the infantry. This consisted of tiny fragments of metal, and was used in roughly the same way as our modern shrapnel.

Gun-carriages

The illustrations show how rapidly the cannon took on the overall appearance that it still retains to this day. The various methods that were used to transport it, however, are less immediately obvious. The depiction of artillery trains on the march found in several works by contemporary artists of the period cannot fail to amaze us, for in most cases the large-calibre cannon are harnessed to – or, more accurately, suspended from – the horse's croup by the trail. So they were trundled along the terribly bumpy roads of the period, balanced in this precarious fashion. The delightful watercolour illustrations in the manuscript by Captain Vasselieu depict the three heaviest guns in the French artillery being hauled along by this curious method. The poor horse harnessed next to the gun had to take the whole weight of the imbalance on his back; however, there were usually between six and twenty-four horses harnessed in front of it, to help it along. There is no sign of any shafts or swingletrees in the detailed drawings we have of these amazing harnesses. If we study the text closely, however, one thing becomes apparent: although the costumes belong to the beginning of the 17th century (the date mentioned in the title of the work), the text accompanying the illustrations is without question taken from old treatises written by La Treille, Vigenère, and Raconis that date back more than forty years. The illustrations were obviously done after the text, and the artist has simply translated the gist of the writing directly into pictures. Another point to note is a drawing of a limber pulled by four horses which the caption labels as 'wheels for raising the cannon'. It seems clear to us from this description that the illustrator did not even know what a limber was for.

Other equally imaginative illustrations have led a good many experts to the wrong conclusions. Thus, for example, certain authorities post-date the use of the limber in England to 1680, yet it is depicted in the work of the great German illustrators like

ARTILLERY (VI)
1. Light gun with built-in caissons (c.1520). The caissons in this illustration (like the one shown in fig. 2) would be used for holding tools, spare parts, rivets, horse-shoes, etc. 2. Light gun with twin falconets (1505). The falconet was the smallest of the 'six calibres of France' that were laid down in the mid-16th century, in the reign of Henri II. The black and red decoration of the gun is typical of the artillery of the Emperor Maximilian I. 3. Loading a gun (1520). On the ground, to the right of the gun, there is a powder-ladle, a ramrod and a swab. The three barrels contain the three ingredients used to make gunpowder – charcoal, sulphur and saltpetre. At this period the gunner still weighed and mixed the powder in the basin lying at his feet just before firing. 4. Light falcon gun with accessories (late 16th century).

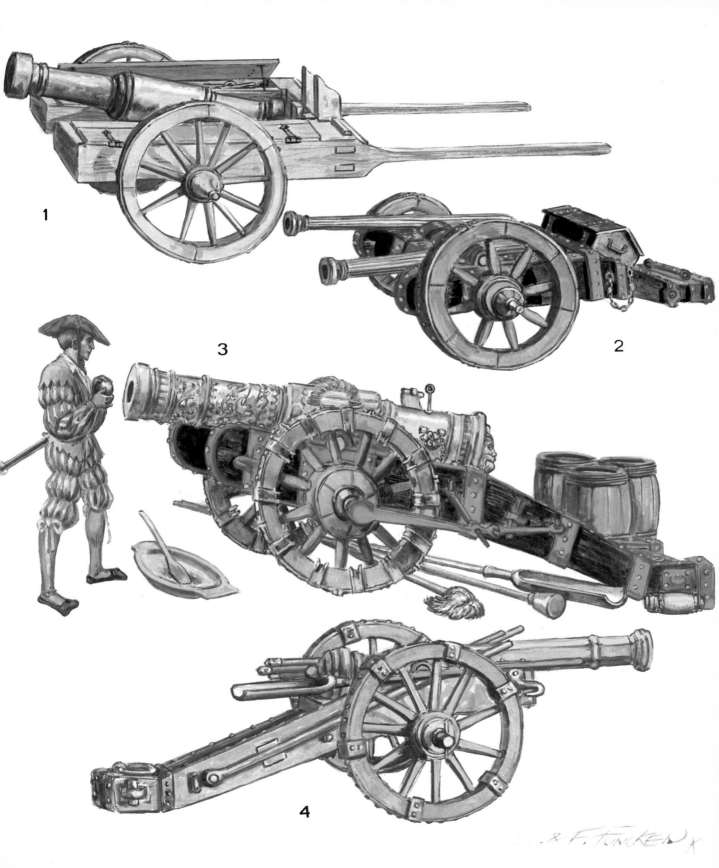

Dürer, Pfintzig, and Glockenthon, and the Italian, Petrarqua, as early as the beginning of the 16th century. Moreover, it is more than likely that this simple little vehicle was already used on the first wheeled cannons that appeared at the end of the previous century, during the reign of Louis XI. After all, horse-drawn transport had been used since time immemorial and had been virtually perfected for some time, notably in Central Europe: in the 15th century the French knight and chronicler Bertrandon de la Broquière brought back a detailed description of the methods of horse-breeding and transportation used there.

The huge number of horses apparently needed to transport such gun-carriages also seems to us to be rather suspect. Figures of thirty to fifty-six horses for one heavy piece are commonly quoted, yet an average-sized draught horse can pull 400 kilos from a stationary position, and four horses can pull a weight of 1 tonne over a distance of 40 kilometres in nine hours. The heaviest cannon shown in Vasselieu's illustrations weighed 4000 kilos, and so could probably have been pulled by a far smaller number of horses.

Fortifications

Few changes occurred in the field of fortifications during the hundred years that followed the introduction of the cannon apart from the conversion of loopholes, which were adapted to take firearms.

In the 15th century people began building and equipping artillery casemates. The ventilation in these structures was usually inadequate, and sustained firing must have been impossible because of the build-up of highly dangerous carbon monoxide gas released by the explosions. The vast majority of feudal lords gave up the attempt to convert their fortresses to withstand artillery fire, and so they were left vulnerable to attack. By contrast most fortified towns, in particular border towns with 'Roman' walls, managed to adapt successfully to the new style of siege warfare. Walls were lowered and made thicker so as to be able to support the weight of heavy artillery. These massive banks of earth were reinforced by solid masonry and flanked with low casemates, while the foot of the towers was reinforced with earth. In the Low Countries water was used to flood the base of low ramparts made of flattened earth. Elsewhere rivers were occasionally diverted – Padua, Sienna, Metz, and Vienna all used this method of defence to withstand heavy artillery attacks.

The techniques used by besieging armies also underwent some development. Devices like sapping trenches, side planking, and battery platforms now began to take shape; these were later to be perfected by Vauban.[1]

This marks the end of another in our series of surveys of military life through the ages. No doubt the knight and the soldier have not always been shown here in the idealized light we usually portray them in. Nevertheless, whether they were scoundrels or legendary heroes, it was they who first discovered the meaning of the word 'nation'.

Mais vous n'avez eu que de coups,
De la pluie, du vent et des poux
Dont vous n'étiez pas à votre aise!

(And you've had nothing but
wind, rain, blows, and lice
which didn't please you too much!)

So sang old soldiers on their way home from war, without in the least suspecting that they were in the process of building Europe.

---

[1] Despite these advances astrology was still heavily relied on by besieging armies. Michel de Nostradamus, the second son of the famous astrologer, was summarily executed in 1574 outside Le Pouzin en Vivarais for trying to start a fire in the town. He had predicted it would be burnt down, but in fact it was captured intact.

ARTILLERY (VII)
1. Transporting a heavy-calibre mortar with two of its cannonballs (c.1510). 2 and 3. Method of elevation using a capstan; shown on two types of gun dating from 1550.

INDEX